A Plantation Mistress on
the Eve of the Civil War

Women's Diaries and Letters of
the Nineteenth-Century South

A Plantation Mistress on the Eve of the Civil War

*The Diary of
Keziah Goodwyn Hopkins Brevard,
1860–1861*

Edited by John Hammond Moore

UNIVERSITY OF SOUTH CAROLINA PRESS

All illustrations—except "Keziah's World," compiled by John H. Moore— are the property of Theodore J. Hopkins, Jr., whose grandfather English Hopkins managed Keziah's properties after the Civil War. The photo of the Veal survey is the work of Charles Gay, South Caroliniana Library.

Copyright © 1993 University of South Carolina Press

Published in Columbia, South Carolina, by the University of South Carolina Press

Published 1993
First Paperback Edition 1996

Manufactured in the United States of America

99 98 97   5 4 3

ISBN 1–57003–125–8

Library of Congress Catalog Card Number: 92–23308

Contents

Illustrations

Series Editor's Introduction

A Plantation Mistress on the Eve of the Civil War is the sixth volume in an ongoing series of women's diaries and letters of the nineteenth-century South. In this series published by the University of South Carolina Press will be a number of never-before-published diaries, some collections of unpublished correspondence, and a few reprints of published diaries—a potpourri of nineteenth-century women's writings.

The Women's Diaries and Letters of the Nineteenth-Century South Series enables women to speak for themselves, providing readers with a rarely opened window into Southern society before, during, and after the American Civil War. The significance of these letters and journals lies not only in the personal revelations and the writing talents of these women authors but also in the range and versatility of their contents. Taken together these publications will tell us much about the heyday and the fall of the Cotton Kingdom, the mature years of the "peculiar institution," the war years, and the adjustment of the South to a new social order following the defeat of the Confederacy. Through these writings the reader will also be presented with firsthand accounts of everyday life and social events, courtships and marriages, family life and travels, religion and education, and the life-and-death matters that made up the ordinary and extraordinary world of the nineteenth-century South.

A Plantation Mistress on the Eve of the Civil War is a brief but revealing diary written between July 22, 1860, and April 15, 1861, by Keziah Goodwyn Hopkins Brevard, a wealthy, fifty-seven-year-old widow who lived about ten miles east of Columbia, South Carolina. Keziah owned four homes, at least three plantations, a grist mill, and over two hundred slaves. Her words reflect a no-nonsense, managerial mind. Between 1844 when she inherited property from her father and her death in 1886 she more than doubled her holdings. Yet despite personal wealth, she cooked, preserved fruit and vegetables, made wine, and took part in household activities. She makes especially interesting comments about the daily routine of operating several households with slaves, personal relations with those slaves and neighbors, and the effect of religion on the local scene.

This journal was compiled during critical months on the eve of the Civil War. Among the events recorded by Keziah are the political campaign and subsequent election of Abraham Lincoln, South

Carolina's secession convention, and the attack on Fort Sumter. Keziah's diary is especially interesting in that it chronicles the events and political climate prior to the war, stopping where better-known writers such as Emma Holmes and Mary Boykin Chesnut start their diaries.

Carol Bleser
July 1991

Acknowledgments

The assistance of several individuals closely associated with Lower Richland has made the task of preparing this diary for publication much less formidable than it might have been. Among them are Laura Jervey Hopkins, whose *Lower Richland Planters*, published in 1976, provides considerable information concerning Keziah's circle of friends and relatives; her nephew, Theodore Jervey Hopkins, Jr.; and A. Mason Gibbes, owner of Alwehav, Keziah's Sand Hills home. John A. Middleton, now in the midst of an awesome genealogical exercise involving his ancestors, men and women once owned by Keziah Goodwyn Hopkins Brevard, also kindly shared his research with me.

A Plantation Mistress on
the Eve of the Civil War

Introduction

The pages that follow are concerned largely with the perplexing problem of relationships faced on the eve of the Civil War by Keziah G. H. Brevard, a fifty-seven-year-old widow living in Richland District, the heart of South Carolina. These include day-to-day dealings with slaves and neighbors, dilemmas posed by the secession crisis, and for Keziah—above all else—relations with her God. Virtually alone in the world and often the only white person at her Sand Hills home in the Midlands ten miles east of Columbia, now called Alwehav, Keziah used a little memorandum book to record casual thoughts and keep track of a great variety of matters. These encompassed everything from dramatic events on the national scene to small sums of money loaned to various individuals, including slaves; the number of eggs collected each day; preserves put by for the winter; bags of flour and bottles of wine on hand; clothing and tobacco parceled out to slaves; inventories of counterpanes and hams; gardening notations; and, on one occasion, a month-long tally of work done by Sylvia, an especially troublesome slave, whom Keziah slyly refers to as "the great lady." In all, about one hundred and sixty pages of diary entries are interspersed with lists and notations that she called her "domestic concerns." Most of these random matters, since they interrupt the chronological flow, are not reproduced in the text that follows.

This little book, which covers the period from 22 July 1860 to 15 April 1861, also contains several poems, recollections of a dancing master, bits on family genealogy, a description of Adams Hill (a summer colony located near Alwehav during the early decades of the nineteenth century), and lamentations concerning the decline of Beulah Baptist Church as well-to-do planters of Lower Richland, especially her Adams cousins, embraced the Episcopal faith. In addition to being a record of household activity and a collection of scattered personal comment, this volume served in quiet moments as both companion and confessional, a retreat where Keziah could discuss her innermost thoughts with herself.

This is, then, a chronological account of how one plantation mistress viewed events both great and small during the forty weeks leading up to the Civil War. There is an entry for each day and little evidence of erasure or subsequent revision. The most momentous events of those weeks, matters of national importance, were three in number: the political campaign leading to the election of Abraham Lincoln in November 1860, South Carolina's secession convention held the following month in Columbia and then in Charleston, and the relentless drumbeat of crisis culminating in the attack upon Fort Sumter in April of 1861.

It is readily apparent that this Midlands plantation mistress, owner of over two hundred slaves, reacted strongly to the political ferment of 1860. Entries during the month of October—nearly twice as voluminous as those of August and September—become outright assaults upon "the rabble of the North." Her words of 13, 24, and 28 October fully prepare the reader for the emotional outburst of 9 November: "Oh My God!!! This morning heard that Lincoln was elected—I had prayed that God would thwart his election in some way & I prayed for my *Country*." The act of secession, although Keziah thought it "rash," failed to stir similar passions—perhaps because that news had to compete with Yuletide festivities, a house guest (grandnephew Jesse Goodwyn Ross from Louisiana, a student at the University of North Carolina, who would die of war wounds in Richmond in 1864), and intermittent fears of serious illness. This vague malady, variously described as sore throat, shoulder pains, nervous rheumatism, and neuralgia, may have been inspired by the declining health of half nephew James Hopkins Adams, who was suffering from cancer.

Nor did the firing on Fort Sumter elicit extensive comment because Keziah's diary ends abruptly on 15 April 1861. But the relatively long entries of January and February—much more verbose than those of other months—are quite another matter. It is during these weeks in early 1861 that Keziah wrestles privately with the morality of secession and slavery, all the while beseeching the Almighty to end this impasse. At times she almost shifts responsibility for whatever ensues to God himself: "If thou withhold thy aid we are undone . . . forsake not the works of *thine own hands:* we are thine—bless the Lord, *we are thine* . . . spare us Lord—& see if we cannot, will not serve thee better." In the process, Keziah analyzes the burden of being a slave owner, calling to mind the constant demands "servants" make upon master and mistress and giving voice to those ever-present but rarely expressed fears: slave revolt and miscegenation.

The importance of this diary lies first and foremost in its timeliness. Keziah's words, in truth, can be read as a prelude to what better known writers such as Emma Holmes and Mary Boykin Chesnut had to say concerning the war years. Both of these fellow South Carolinians start their diaries about where Keziah stops.[1] In fact, the first words of Emma Holmes on 13 February 1861 are "How I wish I had kept a journal during the last three months of great political changes." Five days later, Mrs. Chesnut began sketching her famous portrait of Confederate society, and each of these authors opens with a brief summary of what happened during the winter of 1860–1861.

Unlike Holmes and Chesnut, Keziah did not have a front row seat in Charleston during the exciting spring of 1861, but she had an opportunity to witness what they did. On 24 March, as another meeting of the secession convention was getting under way in Charleston, Mrs. James Hopkins Adams asked Keziah if she wished to go to the "Holy City," but she declined. Had Keziah accepted this invitation, she certainly would have encountered Mrs. Chesnut, who, like Jane Margaret Adams, accompanied her husband to Charleston. Two days later Mary Chesnut wrote of a crowded train ride from Camden to the coast and told of meeting the Adamses at dinner. During the weeks that followed, their names, as well as that of their son Warren, appeared from time to time in Chesnut's diary.

For us, generations later, it is probably just as well that Keziah stayed home. Actually she seemed irritated by the sudden proposal to go to Charleston: "now this is a pretty way to act—how was I to arrange on sunday to get off before day monday." As result of Keziah staying at home, we have a far more typical reaction to what was happening during the first months of 1861. Here was a woman past middle age living in a rural setting with only rumor and innate feeling as guides at a crucial juncture in her life and that of her nation. Keziah apparently read newspapers infrequently and rarely met with individuals able to shed light upon what was transpiring, though at times she expressed the desire to do so. For ninety troubled days (January through March) she prayed strenuously for God's help, pondered the dilemmas presented by secession, and weighed the chances for peace or war. Most of her prayers end with the words "Lord save our country." However, as the days pass, it is difficult to know which "country" the Almighty is supposed to save. In any case, on 2 April Keziah concedes strife is inevitable.

> I am sorry our once strong country is now severed & I believe forever—for I see no disposition in the stubborn North to yield

---

1. See John F. Marszalek, ed., *The Diary of Miss Emma Holmes, 1861–1866* (Baton Rouge, 1979); C. Vann Woodward, ed., *Mary Chesnut's Civil War* (New Haven, 1981); and C. Vann Woodward and Elizabeth Muhlenfeld, [eds.], *The Private Mary Chesnut: The Unpublished Civil War Diaries* (New York, 1984).

> any thing from advantage—& the South thought she would
> make the North succumb to her—*I* never thought it—& have
> ever thought we have began troubles for ourselves & cannot see
> how we are to be one tittle better off than we were—if all the
> South had gone united we might have maintained ourselves—
> but six states only—we are doomed I fear to be the division of
> the Old United States. O my God *help us—help us—*

Yet these diary entries, like all others, range from the most serious issues before the country to the mundane and trivial as Keziah talks about weather, farming, financial matters, and events in the neighborhood where she lives. Unlike Emma Holmes and Mary Chesnut, this childless widow was beset by numerous daily responsibilities that could not be shared with husband or offspring. An overseer cared for two large plantations in Lower Richland, but Keziah personally directed affairs at her Sand Hills home (which produced some crops each year) and looked after her Columbia town house as well. Of especial significance is that Keziah Brevard actually lived *with* her slaves much of each day. They were both servants and companions. This does not imply unusual affection, merely that a dozen or so household staff and field hands rounded out the "family" she did not have.

Taken as a whole, what is now merely a handful of loose, unbound pages provides a remarkable glimpse of day-to-day life in the "big house" as war clouds gather. Obvious necessity to keep track of intricate details in a plantation world and the skill with which these entries are recorded lead one to believe that Keziah compiled many such journals during her lifetime; however, this apparently is the only one that has survived—and occasional comments reveal she fully intended that it should. Also, several of her minor financial transactions are marked officially closed after April of 1861.

At her death the diary passed into the hands of relatives living in Louisiana. In June of 1971, A. Mason Gibbes, who now owns Alwehav, placed a typed transcript of its contents in the South Carolinian Library at the University of South Carolina, and a few years later a slightly different version was printed privately by the Hopkins family. Until 1988, when Miss Laura Jervey Hopkins presented the original diary to the same library, researchers have been forced to rely upon the typed transcript, which, like the printed version, differs somewhat from the original text. Now, published for the first time is this complete diary of a prominent plantation mistress written on the eve of the Civil War.

In her struggles during the twilight of the Old South, Keziah Brevard had several distinct advantages, among them, a keen mind, shrewd business sense, relatively good health, and substantial financial resources. She was, in fact, perhaps the region's prize catch as a young girl and, according to family legend, even as a middle-aged widow attracted at least one admirer. However, when informed by relatives that, under the terms of her father's will, whatever Keziah inherited would remain within the family, his ardor cooled and the pursuit came to an end.

Keziah Goodwyn Hopkins was born in 1803, the daughter of Keziah and James Hopkins, at what is now known as Oldfield plantation, then called Cabin Branch. This property, located about nine miles southeast of Columbia, was granted to John Hopkins of Hanover County, Virginia, in the mid–1700s and still is owned by the Hopkins family. Her mother, widow of Jesse Goodwyn, had three children by her first marriage, the most important on the local scene being Sarah, wife of Columbia merchant Ainsley Hall. (See the genealogical charts on page 6.) By the second marriage Keziah Hopkins gave birth to five children—three boys who died in childhood, Keziah, and a younger sister, Caroline. Keziah's father apparently was trained in medicine, but never practiced, choosing instead to devote his life to family and business matters such as planting, acquisition of land, and investments. In the 1820s the young Hopkins women married brothers from North Carolina. Caroline had two sons, but both died young, and she herself failed to recover from the birth of her second child in 1828. Keziah had no children and thus, upon the death of her father in 1844, became sole heir to his substantial holdings in Lower Richland.

Her nearest blood relatives, following the death of her mother in 1840 and that of her father four years later, included her half brother Jesse (1793–1862), who moved to Louisiana when Keziah was about nine years old, and the son of her half sister Mary (1789–1813). Another half sister, Sarah Hall, who figures prominently in these pages as "Sister," had no children; following Ainsley Hall's death in 1823, Sarah sold her Columbia mansion (now restored as the Robert Mills House) to the Columbia Theological Seminary and moved to Bellewood, a property about nine miles east of town en route to Sumter. There, somewhat mentally disturbed, she became a recluse and was cared for by Keziah during her last years.

Her half sister Mary's only child, James Hopkins Adams—governor of South Carolina from 1854 to 1856—married Jane Margaret

The Goodwyn and Hopkins Families

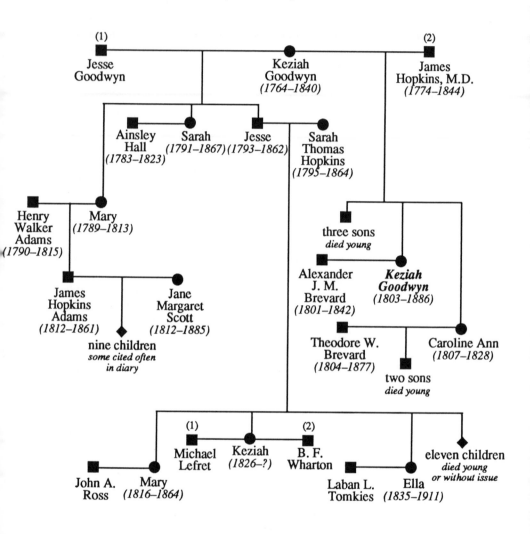

Scott, a native of Lower Richland. James, his wife, and their children often were guests of Keziah Brevard, especially four daughters ranging in ages from nineteen to ten in 1860: Jane Margaret, Laura Keziah, Ellen Tree, and Caroline (Carry) Hopkins. But Keziah's closest friend was her "Cousin Emma" (1808–1868), wife of General William Hopkins (1805–1863).[2] Emma and her children, among them, David, James, English, Amy, and Sarah (Sally) are mentioned frequently in the diary; and, following the deaths of their parents, Amy and Sarah lived with Keziah for a time at Alwehav. English Hopkins became manager of Keziah's properties during the postwar years.

"Kizzie," as she was called within the family, probably was educated at nearby Minervaville Academy and at Columbia Female Academy operated by Dr. Elias Marks, the man who in 1828 established a well-known institute for girls in Barhamville, a little community located northeast of Columbia. She undoubtedly visited her relatives the Ainsley Halls during these years and perhaps at times even lived with them. If so, Keziah got a brief course in how quickly marital ties can become frayed. Her half sister Sarah's marriage apparently was happy enough until she discovered a letter indicating Hall was romantically involved with someone else. To Sarah's dismay, her husband not only admitted the relationship but defended the "other woman." It was, he said, entirely his fault. Sarah appealed to her stepfather, who ruled out divorce since such a step was rarely contemplated in those days and would stain the family name. Admittedly, this turn of events was highly embarrassing, for Hall was a close friend of numerous members of the Hopkins and Goodwyn families. Only his death in 1823 at a relatively young age—he was forty—resolved this impasse, and his will, a complex document indeed, reveals he provided handsomely for his widow and left bequests to many of her relatives, including Keziah and her father.

Keziah's marital story, although somewhat different, also encompassed grief and disappointment, possibly even physical abuse. In April of 1827 she married Alexander Joseph McLean Brevard, whose father owned considerable land in North Carolina and earned fame as a pioneer iron entrepreneur in Lincoln County. Young Brevard, who went by the name of Joseph, attended South Carolina College from 1818 to 1820, but did not graduate. By the mid-20s Keziah's sister, Caroline, was already the wife of Theodore Brevard, Joseph's brother, and the family had close ties with Brevard cousins in nearby

---

2. William, Emma, and Keziah were, respectively, the children of three Hopkins brothers—Thomas, John, and James—thus first cousins.

Camden, so there were several routes by which any casual association spawned by college days in Columbia or regional social gatherings could have blossomed into romance.

Joseph, two years older than Keziah, took his bride to the Charlotte–Lincoln County area of North Carolina, where they set up housekeeping, and he served a term (November 1827–January 1828) as one of two representatives from Lincoln County in the lower house of the state legislature. But the marriage soon was troubled, according to Hopkins heirs, by the groom's excessive drinking, and within a year or so Keziah had had enough. One day she suddenly packed her things, ordered her carriage, and came home to father. Joseph followed on horseback; however, in contrast to the usual pleading for his wife to return home, he decided to remain at Oldfield. Just when these dramatic developments occurred is not known, but recording of the elder Brevard's will in Columbia in October of 1831 indicates that son Joseph, one of the executors, was living in Richland District by that date.

During the ensuing decade Joseph Brevard spent several months as a patient in the South Carolina State Hospital, then called simply the Lunatic Asylum. Official records, now at the State Archives, reveal that in the first instance (27 November 1835–26 January 1836) he was suffering from what a doctor diagnosed as "monomania"—a mental disorder dominated by a single theme or idea. He was, this physician wrote, "jealous of his wife & deems himself in honour bound to find out her delinquincy & challenge her paramour." This gentleman added that Brevard was "very dyspeptic" but, following several weeks of treatment, had been released. Shortly before he returned home, however, his father-in-law, James Hopkins, and Jesse Goodwyn posted bond with local authorities and became legal guardians of Joseph Brevard's estate.

Five years later Keziah's husband was hospitalized once more, a physician summing up his condition in this fashion:

> He has been deranged for some time, but kept at home—was formerly in the asylum & dismissed as cured . . . he was admitted on 15 Sep^t 1841—Is very dyspeptic, imagines that every one about him has tried to poison him & he is not willing to eat any food that is brought by his keepers—upon attending to his general health he improved very much—but his Friends were afraid of taking him home—In February his health gave way, he had frequent attacks of fever accompanied by gastric & interic irritability which prostrated him very much—removed by friends on 20 April 1842.

Joseph Brevard died on 1 June 1842 at the home of his father-in-law. By an agreement Keziah concluded with his family on 30 November 1842, she relinquished $2,000 left to her in his will, as well as claim to anything he owned in North Carolina. In return, she was allowed to keep books, furniture, and property belonging to her late husband within South Carolina, which apparently included a few slaves.

Some years earlier, perhaps upon the death of her mother in 1840, Keziah and Joseph had moved to her father's Sand Hills home, which, after James Hopkins died in 1844, became the widow Brevard's principal residence.[3] As the diary reveals, she referred to this estate as Mt. Ed or Mt. Trouble, depending upon her mood, and once even considered calling an enlarged plantation house Fontainebleau. This property, surrounded by huge magnolias, live oaks, and exotic trees and shrubs planted by her father, originally was a spacious cottage built about 1815. Following her father's death, Keziah had that building moved several hundred yards to a new site and joined to it a handsome two-story structure containing large rooms with thirteen-foot ceilings, a wide entrance hall, and porches typical of the period.

Since Keziah was not one to spend money frivolously, expansion of her country home (c. 1847) and simultaneous purchase of a Columbia town house located at the southwest corner of Blanding and Bull streets raise questions that cannot be fully answered. Court records indicate Keziah paid $2,150 for the Columbia property, and work done at her Sand Hills home (moving an old cottage and adding to it virtually another structure) undoubtedly cost even more. She clearly had some goal in mind. The best explanation is that, following the deaths of mother, husband, and father in less than four years, this forty-five-year-old, childless matron felt a natural urge to expand her social horizons—to get out more, see people, do things. Anyone who walks through Alwehav today quickly realizes it was built for entertaining large groups of people.

But that was not to be. Perhaps years spent caring for elderly parents and a demented husband forged habits and attitudes not easily changed, or it may be that Keziah always favored a quiet existence and only fleetingly dreamed of playing hostess on a grand scale. Significantly, passages in her diary reveal a lack of social

---

3. During Keziah's lifetime this Sand Hills home sometimes was called the Brevard Place or Kizzieville. In 1904, when Caroline Adams LeConte acquired the property, it became known as Alwehav.

confidence when compared with various contemporaries such as sister-in-law Peggy Brevard. In any case, Keziah now had the responsibility of managing a large agricultural operation, a task she apparently found more appealing than giving parties and making small talk over tea and cakes.

By the will of James Hopkins, Keziah inherited everything he owned, subject to two special provisions: if his daughter had no heirs "of her body," then all of the property was to go to blood relations upon her death, and her actions relative to this property were subject to the approval of four trustees named by her father. Any doubts James may have harbored concerning the managerial skills of his daughter were ill-founded, for her diary reveals a competent, no-nonsense mind capable of making decisions, formulating plans, and carrying them out.

According to the 1850 census, Keziah was operating two "farms" consisting of 2,600 acres valued at $22,500. On these properties she had 6 horses, 20 mules, 90 cattle, 42 sheep, and 185 swine—livestock worth $2,610. In 1849–1850 she produced 7,073 bushels of corn, 525 bushels of oats, 45 pounds of wool, 700 bushels of peas and beans, 1,700 bushels of sweet potatoes, 200 pounds of butter, 43 tons of hay, and home manufactures with an estimated value of $180. She also ginned 190 bales of cotton and slaughtered animals worth $420. In the decade that followed, Keziah purchased at least ten pieces of nearby property, more than doubling her holdings, while maintaining a creditable output of cotton, corn, wool, and sweet potatoes. By 1860 she owned some 6,000 acres of land, her slave force had grown from 180 to 209, and she had added rice (1,200 pounds) and honey ($175 worth) to her annual harvest of foodstuffs.

In essence Keziah Brevard's realm consisted of four distinct units: the Sand Hills residence (the present Alwehav), her birthplace a few miles to the south, Mill Place, and the Columbia town house. The diary indicates that about twenty slaves, young and old, lived with Keziah in the Sand Hills and carried on household duties and some farming operations. A few more slaves cared for the town property and Mill Place (today called Adams Pond), but the center of greatest activity was Oldfield, then referred to as Cabin Branch, a name shared by several other plantations in the same general area. There a hundred or so able-bodied slaves worked under the supervision of overseer Abraham Rawlinson. Throughout the diary, when Keziah mentions "the plantation" she is talking about Cabin Branch, which she sometimes refers to as "home," a term occasionally applied to her Sand Hills property as well.

The most important of these holdings was Cabin Branch, much augmented by a decade of expansion, for it provided the cotton, corn, wheat, hams, lard, and sausage that sustained life throughout Keziah's little kingdom. At the other end of the scale, at least in the eyes of its owner, was the town house at Bull and Blanding. Despite whatever plans Keziah once may have had for extended sojourns there, by 1860 she viewed Columbia only as a place to transact business, buy plantation supplies, and perhaps attend church. Her idea of a good time was a relaxed family dinner at home in the Sand Hills such as she hosted on 27 July 1860. Ten relatives, young and old, enjoyed a bountiful repast of ham, goose, mutton (roasted and boiled), cabbage, rice, beets, Irish potatoes, and tomatoes (cooked and uncooked). For dessert they had apple dumplings and "soft" peaches. To a lesser degree, she derived some pleasure from tea and conversation with neighbors. In November of 1860 she wrote of a gathering at the home of ex-governor James Hopkins Adams, son of her half sister, at which she met Mrs. H., "a Charleston lady yet her manner is very natural."

Now nearly sixty years of age, Keziah liked to garden, preserve fruits and vegetables, take an accounting of all the foodstuffs on hand, and make wine by the gallon—some of which, to her distress, occasionally turned to vinegar. Frugal, but not parsimonious, she once characterized her family as "good, plain, unpretending people," and that description seems valid enough. As noted, following the death of her father she enlarged her Sand Hills home, but she built no grand structure such as Kensington or Magnolia, two stunning antebellum mansions that still stand in Lower Richland.

Like any good farmer, the widow Brevard kept an eye on the weather, and almost every diary entry has something to say about rain, sunshine, clouds, wind, and temperature. She also looked after the needs of those who worked her land, taking special interest in the welfare of her household slaves. When houseboys Ned and Dick had to help pick cotton, she expressed concern that they could not "stand the sun as the field hands do" and personally nursed little Harrison, son of another slave, during his final illness, even bundling up the black youngster and taking him for rides in her carriage.

Despite kind thoughts and good deeds, Keziah's religious life defies easy analysis. Born into a world of relaxed morality, a time when church activity was not well organized in the Midlands and drinking rampant, she clearly embraced the emotional pietism of her childhood. By mid-century Keziah invoked the mercy of God often and sought His guidance almost daily, yet she rarely attended Sunday services, although frequently wrote in the pages of her diary that she

wished she had done so. As a bride she joined a Presbyterian congregation in North Carolina and more than two decades later (7 April
1851) transferred her membership to the First Presbyterian Church
in Columbia, noting on her application that she was living in a set-
tlement of Baptists "with whom she was not disposed to unite." At
the same time she mourned the decline of Beulah Church, a local
Baptist institution long associated with her family, helped pay the
minister's salary, and spoke scornfully of Adams cousins who had
"gone clear over to the Episcopalians outwardly." The pages of the
Southern Christian Advocate (1860–1861) reveal that she also contributed $20 a year to the Congaree Mission of the Methodist Church, a
facility located on Gill's Creek in Lower Richland.

Keziah, like everyone, was a product of her times. The religious
revivalism of the early 1800s affected her thoughts, as did the widely
touted paternalism of master toward slave. She wanted desperately to
be respected and even loved by those she owned and often tried to
cultivate their affection. Little is said in this diary about disciplinary
measures, but it is difficult to see how a widow in her late fifties could
exert much pressure upon her "servants" without endangering the
rapport she sought. In fact, when Jim distressed her, she considered
asking her nephew to attend to the matter. On several occasions she
paid for destruction wreaked upon a slave's crop by hogs and cattle
even though her animals were not at fault. These are "my poor," she
commented, so why not help them?

Admittedly, the widow Brevard was cast in a difficult role—alone
in the world, mistress of several plantations, and yet frequently working side by side with individuals she could sell to new owners, if she
wished to do so. Together they cooked, strained lard, parceled out
clothing, and performed numerous other plantation chores. One can
only conjecture as to what sort of relationships developed. It was unusual enough for a woman to actually *run* a plantation herself, but
here was a mistress who was trying to be friend, manager, and, in a
sense, something of a co-worker at the same time. Unlike most of her
contemporaries, Keziah occasionally ventured into the kitchen as
more than mere observer and joined personally in various tasks.
"Making cake, expecting Mrs. R. & Miss R. to dine with me." "I
finished Mrs. Willson's cake." "Sylvia & myself had commenced
making potatoe pudding." "Mary & myself made potatoe custard to
day." "Fanny—John & myself put seventy two new hams in bags."
This owner of over two hundred slaves cooked, cared for hams, and
so on because she found pleasure in such pursuits. As she once re-
marked, "I have enjoyed out door work this morning." Keziah

Brevard may have understood the multiple roles she was playing, but most of her "servants" probably did not.

One minor incident illustrates the mental confusion that perhaps resulted from such close, day-by-day contact. On 9 March, Keziah gave her cook some cold turkey and asked her to prepare "a little soup for my dinner." Through some misunderstanding, other members of the household staff ate the soup. Keziah was furious and scolded the cook, who retorted she wanted to return to her former owner and vowed she would starve rather than eat anything "she cooked for me again." On the surface this seems to be an unusually violent reaction; but, of course, we do not know what form the "scolding" took or what had been going on between Keziah and her cook in days or hours prior to the causal request to make soup.

Even when relations were harmonious, Keziah, like most wealthy people accustomed to having their own way in all matters, knew precisely what the response of her slaves should be to any kind act on her part. When that response was not forthcoming, a slave was, in her view, "impudent." Although Keziah never fully explains this impudence in the pages of her diary, it seems to have encompassed a multitude of indiscretions such as disobeying orders, kicking another slave, singing a hymn while working in the kitchen, and picking garden produce without specific permission to do so. Her greatest shortcoming in relations with her slaves, Keziah concedes, was a lack of patience, and on numerous occasions she pleads with the Almighty for guidance and help. Early in February of 1861, for example, she wrote, "I have sinned this day grumbling with my poor negroes, I ought to have more patience."

With the advent of war, the religious philosophy of this plantation mistress encountered an acute dilemma. If God, as she firmly believed, was all-powerful, all-knowing, and the importation of thousands of Africans to South Carolina was perhaps divinely ordained, then the election of Abraham Lincoln and the breakup of the United States of America also could be part of the heavenly scheme of things. In fact, pressures bearing down upon her beloved state and the new Confederacy might be nothing more than retribution for past sins. Keziah, troubled by these thoughts, took a dim view of secession. In her opinion it was coming much too fast and was too disorganized—pregnant with seeds of still greater fragmentation.

While Keziah Brevard embraced pietism and paternalism with obvious fervor, two other prominent themes of her age—temperance and emancipation—failed to arouse similar passions. Considering the problems her husband allegedly had with drink, her wine-making activity appears somewhat puzzling. However, it is quite possible that, as some individuals do today, Keziah drew firm distinction between light fermented wine and distilled liquor. As for the emancipation of slaves, it is no surprise to discover she held contradictory views. In her eyes, Northern abolitionists were nothing but fanatical "cut-throats," yet this mistress of over two hundred blacks claimed on at least one occasion that she, too, wanted to end human bondage—but, again, only on *her* terms. Freedom for blacks was impossible, Keziah writes with conviction, so long as so many of them remain "in our midst yet." "A degraded population," she once lamented, "is a curse to a country."

As one reads Keziah's fervent prayers to the Almighty, mingled with criticism of slavery and secession, the arrival and departure of guests, a tally of wine bottles stored away, changes in the weather, and the score of mice being trapped, distinct personality traits emerge. As observed earlier, she was a shrewd businesswoman who paid close attention to detail, an individual with a largely pragmatic, practical view of the world. Nevertheless, she could be troubled by dreams and often tried to evaluate their true meaning, if any. In a male-dominated society of agriculture and finance, she was a rousing success; and, although Keziah Brevard never pointed a finger directly at the male of the species, her railings against the sins and evil nature of *mankind* come close to the mark at times. Certainly her experience in marriage and that of "Sister" won this widow the right to be wary of husbands and all men in general. In addition, her abhorrence of Columbia and avowed preference for the solitude of the rural realm where she ruled supreme round out the picture of a plantation mistress eager to be truly independent.

Identifying the people of that realm would have been virtually impossible without the assistance of *Lower Richland Planters*, published in 1976 by Laura Jervey Hopkins. Nonrelatives, friends, and neighbors mentioned by Keziah usually can be identified with the help of census rolls. Among such individuals are Irish-born Jane S. Jones, age seventy-nine, mother of Mrs. James Hopkins Adams; Abraham Rawlinson, overseer of Keziah's Cabin Branch plantation; and Duncan Ray, a well-to-do planter-physician who lived in Lower Richland. However, Thomas Walker, the man who compiled these statistics on the eve of the Civil War, was—to say the least—casual in his approach to the task of counting noses. Comparison of his reports with early city directories reveals, for example, that in Columbia he began by strolling down Main Street and recording whatever shopkeepers told him. As a result, some names appear in both city and county, some not at all. And Walker's list of rural households is equally suspect, for the sequence of household numbers often is a confused mass of duplication and omission.

Nevertheless, despite such errors, it is apparent that regional population declined somewhat during the 1850s, largely because of outmigration of both slaves and masters. According to Walker's returns, the number of Richland District residents fell from 20,243 to 18,307, and almost all of this loss was black. The white aggregate rose slightly (6,764 to 6,863), while the black population fell from 13,479 to 11,444. Meanwhile, although the community was struggling with relatively hard economic times, Columbia's population grew from 6,060 to 8,052.

Changes such as these had marked effect on the plantations of Lower Richland. In 1850 various members of the influential Adams family owned 1,100 slaves; ten years later they were masters of only 800. On the eve of war Frank Hampton owned 260, the William Clarkson estate 210, and Keziah Brevard 209; for, as noted, in these lean seasons this remarkable woman managed carefully and bought up land as her neighbors departed to try their luck in Florida, Texas, and other far places.[4]

Insofar as possible, the diary that follows has been reproduced as written, complete with what may be considered errors in spelling and capricious capitalization. For clarity, however, material occasionally has been inserted in brackets, and punctuation added in the form of dashes (much favored by Keziah), as well as commas, periods, and apostrophes normally used in contractions or to express possession. Most of her sentences, it might be noted, lack concluding periods or question marks. Abbreviations such as "E" for Emma and "Col" for Columbia have not been spelled out, unless so doing seems to make the text more readable. In such cases, insertions appear in brackets.

One might conclude from this diary that Keziah G. H. Brevard spent many of her days alone, but that is far from true. She was alone only in the sense that she often lacked the company of white people, for Sylvia, Rosanna, Mary, Ned, Tom, and Dorcas—to name a few of the Sand Hills servants—always were nearby; and, as her words reveal, visits to and from relatives and friends were frequent indeed.

---

4. For another view of life in Lower Richland in the 1850s, see the unpublished diary of Dr. Samuel Leland at the South Caroliniana Library. Leland, son of a professor at the Columbia Theological Seminary, was trying to build up a practice as a plantation doctor, but in 1859 he gave up and moved to Cass County, Georgia.

Yet she could feel lonely at times, especially when she compared her lot with that of other women who had a husband and the companionship of children and grandchildren, families that, in her opinion, helped them live their youth once more. Keziah, on the other hand, considered herself "a blank."

But enough of probing, reflecting, and analysis. It is time to let this indomitable plantation mistress speak for herself and her world during the exciting months when Richland District and South Carolina were drifting toward secession, independence, and war.

Cast

Keziah's Friends and Relatives

James Hopkins Adams (1812–1861), only son of Keziah's half sister Mary, governor of South Carolina 1854–1856.

Jane Margaret Scott Adams (1812–1885), wife of James Hopkins Adams.

Mary Elizabeth Boykin (1812–1877), sister of William Hopkins and wife of Lemuel Boykin of nearby Kershaw District.

Caroline Mays Brevard (1811–1892), second wife of Theodore W. Brevard, who first married Keziah's younger sister, also named Caroline.

Margaret ("Peggy") Conner Brevard, widow of J. Franklin Brevard (1788–1829), Keziah's brother-in-law.

Sarah Cooke Goodwyn Hall (1791–1867), half sister of Keziah and widow of Columbia merchant Ainsley Hall (1783–1823), often referred to in the diary as "Sister."

Amy Goodwyn Hopkins (1845–1896), daughter of William and Emma Hopkins. She and her sister Sarah lived with Keziah for a time in the 1870s.

Emma Goodwyn Hopkins (1808–1868), wife of William Hopkins, Keziah's cousin and closest friend.

English Hopkins (1842–1918), son of William and Emma Hopkins, manager of Keziah's properties in the 1870s and 1880s.

Frances ("Fanny") Tucker Hopkins (1806–1864), widow of David Hopkins, mother of John David and James Tucker Hopkins, the lady who built Magnolia (Wavering Place) in the 1850s. She is often referred to as Mrs. F. M. Hopkins. Her husband, who died in 1836, was a brother of Emma Hopkins.

Sarah ("Sally") Thomas Hopkins (1851–1927), daughter of William and Emma Hopkins.

William Hopkins (1805–1863), often called "General" in the diary. William, his wife Emma, and Keziah were the children of three brothers and thus first cousins.

Jane S. Jones (1782–1866), mother of Mrs. James Hopkins Adams and widow of Samuel Scott and Darling Jones.

Abraham Rawlinson, overseer of Keziah's Cabin Branch plantation.

Duncan Ray (1812–1868), neighbor and well-to-do planter physician.

Cast: Keziah's Friends and Relatives

Sally F. Ray (1821–1899), wife of Duncan Ray.

Jesse Goodwyn Ross, grandson of Keziah's half brother, Jesse Howell Goodwyn. This young man, who grew up in Louisiana, was attending the University of North Carolina when he was Keziah's house guest during Christmas 1860. He subsequently died of war wounds and was buried in Richmond, Virginia.

The Diary of
Keziah Goodwyn Hopkins Brevard,
July 1860–April 1861

July
"I shall sow turnip seed to day."

July 22 At home with sore throat.

22 Sister spent the day with me—clouds & lightning in the afternoon—no rain.

23 Mrs. Rawlinson came to see me—great hopes of rain in the afternoon, terrible looking clouds—a sprinkle of rain.

24 I went to Cabin branch late P.M.—[1]

25 left Cabin branch at 6 O'clock A.M.—came back & went & dined with Emma. Cousin Mary Boykin with her[2]—got home by sun down—clouds kept me in dread all the way—no rain.

26 This day weighed two peaches—together they weighed fourteen ounces, good weight—one weighed one ounce more than the other when balanced— A sprinkle of rain this afternoon late—very dark clouds in the West—we have some change in the temperature—more pleasant tonight. I wish I knew what produced anger in the human body. My God I ask thee for help—yes help to love thy ways & hate all that is not pleasing in thy sight. Lord Jesus my redeemer—again & again I ask for help to be more like thee—

27th Friday Emma—Amy—Sally & English Hopkins—Cousin Mary Boykin—her son Samuel—Frank & little Mary—with John & James Hopkins dined with me to day[3]— I had for dinner

---

1. Keziah originally wrote "A.M." and throughout her diary seemed to confuse designations for morning and afternoon.

2. Mary Elizabeth Boykin (1812–1877), sister of William Hopkins and wife of Lemuel Boykin of Kershaw District, located northeast of Columbia.

3. In addition to Mary Boykin and her three youngest children, this group includes Emma Hopkins and three of her children (Amy, Sally, and English) and John Hopkins (1827–1868) and James Hopkins (1831–1863), sons of Emma's brother David (1802–1836) and Frances ("Fanny") Tucker Hopkins, (1806–1864), the lady who built Magnolia in the mid-1850s. Both John and James were about to depart for new homes in Florida. Emma also had a son named James, who is mentioned later.

One New HAM brought out this morning[4]—roast & boiled mutton, two young geese, last spring goslins, cabbage, rice, tomattos, cooked & not cooked, beets, Irish pota[t]oes & rice—desert Apple dumpling & soft peaches. In the afternoon plenty of clouds, no rain.

28 Late this afternoon—Kate—Laura, Ellen & Carry Adams came—staid to tea—Kate suits me—I love her ways—I love Laura, too, but she is too fussy.[5] Laura don't be angry. Flour. The new flour was sent out yesterday morning—I received 5 bags of New flour each weighing ninety two lb. & one bag of 55—this bag I opened & used out of it for dinner. These bags were first quality flour. 1 bag of 88 lb. second quality. 1 bag of 53 lb. third quality. One bag of 109 lb. last quality.

28 I let Dick have a 100 lb. bag of Old flour to day @ 3.50— We had a little rain this afternoon—I do hope it did good to many. Bottles— Took three bottles from the barrel this night for catsup—28th of July.

29 Sunday At home—a good rain. P.M.

30 Monday This is a very warm afternoon & *lutte*[6]—shower about four O'clock P.M., so close we may have more rain before night. Yesterday in the afternoon we had rain which I hope did some good—but this scorching sun is dreadful on wet things.

31st Last day of July 1860—sure enough last night we had a good season—I shall sow turnip seed to day. Last night I dreamed there was to be a commotion of some kind in Col———— on Tuesday night. This will be Tuesday night—I do hope there will be nothing to correspond with this dream—I don't wish to be superstitious—I want my faith to be strengthened in God through his *son*, my blessed *Saviour*— Lord make my faith so strong that no power shall weaken it. I am thine, I trust wholy thine—if not at present—thou art able to make me so—in thee I trust.

---

4. The terms "brought out" and "came out," used frequently in the diary, refer to food and other materials transferred from the principal plantation, Cabin Branch, to Keziah's home in the Sand Hills.

5. Kate (Katherine Ann Henderson), wife of John Randolph Adams (1834–1875), son of Keziah's half nephew, James Hopkins Adams. Laura, Ellen, and Carry (Caroline) were sisters of John Randolph, whom Keziah sometimes refers to as Randy.

6. Although Keziah later remarks that she does not know foreign languages, this is a French word meaning contested, turbid, or unsettled.

August
"We had a glorious rain."

1st of August This day I went to Wm Hopkins' cabin branch place— We had an abundance of nice melons & some peaches—in the afternoon I left Emma & went to my Cabin branch place— after I got there we had a glorious rain—it came on slowly without thunder & ended a pouring blessed rain for the scorched earth & all animals—man as well as beast needed it.

2 Thursday I went to Col———. Consulted Dr Tally about my throat.[1]

3 Came home—it rained in the sand Hills Thursday evening more than it did on Wednesday—

3 Friday —at home before night, no rain to day.

4 At home, no rain.

5 At home. No preaching convenient.

6 Monday Sowed turnips in the Cow pen—

7 Tuesday —went to see Kate & the children, all well, poor children I do feel deeply for you.[2] Oh my God thou wilt take care of the orphan. We have had a succession of sultry days— Ham. The day I went to Col Thursday the second of August I took one Old Ham & made Fanny (my servant) boil it— English, Amy & self made a hearty dinner, supper & breakfast off it— I brought it home & it has lasted till to day & will last two days longer. Ham. On Monday the 6th of August the wagon came out to bring the last flour & brought out One Old Ham & a New Midling. I have cut the midling—5 bags of No. 1 flour—2 bags of No. 2—1 of seconds—1 grudeons & 4 of bran—[3] Left at home 1 bag No. 1 & 1 No. 2 (a present for Mr. & Mrs. Rawlinson). I also have the bag that

---

1. Dr. A. N. Talley's office was located on the south side of Washington Street between Marion and Sumter streets.

2. Keziah is expressing concern for the failing health of her nephew, James Hopkins Adams, only son of her half sister.

3. These terms describe the quality of milled grain and its by-products: middling (mediocre or low-grade flour), grudeons (coarse meal), and bran (the broken seed coating or husks).

was ground at Goodwyn's Mill.[4] Had cider made yesterday, sent Mrs. Ray one gallon of it.[5] Bottels. Wednesday 8th Aug—took out 6 (six) bottels—from the barrel. On Sunday night the 5th of August I think between midnight & day— I dreamed James H. Adams returned— I thought I was up a stair— I know not where— I saw J. H.—comeing up slowly & looking wearied with a complexion of death— I thought I clasped his hands in mine & exclaimed My God! My God! I thought he said to his wife "Oh you don't know how you cheer me"—it seemed to me he had just come home to his wife.

8th This is a bright morning— I paid Tom Prescott this morning by check, all I owe him for work at my mill place.[6] Check on Commercial Bank. S. C. 260.00

8th
Nine jars of cherries & one tumbler	/60
Two D[itt]o choice Plums	/60
Five Do Rasp[berry] jam	/60
Bowl—Do—jelly	/60
Four of cut nectarines	/60
Four Do Peaches	/60
Seven tumblers of A[pple] jelly	/59
Nine tumblers of B[lack] B[erry] jelly	/59
Six tumblers of Old jelly	

Thursday 9th At home expecting Kate & Laura—Kate—Ellen—came & little Janie spent this day with me[7]—I boiled a ham Dick brought out this morning—left the O[ld] Ham that came out on Monday by the Wagon—

Friday 10 At Home—doing little—

11 Made an early start, hoping to go to the mill—the clouds looked so much like rain I stopped at the plantation awhile— went to Emma's to dinner & remained all night—Henrietta Smith with Amy.[8]

Sunday 12th Came home early—

---

4. Goodwyn's Mill was a pre-Revolutionary facility located on Gill's Creek near what would become Boyden Arbor in the early 1900s.
5. Sally F. Ray (1821–1899), wife of Dr. Duncan Ray.
6. Tom Prescott cannot be identified from census records, but he probably was related to a Sumter District family bearing that same name.
7. "Little Janie" was the two-year-old daughter of John Randolph and Katherine (Kate) Adams.
8. Henrietta Smith, age eleven, may have been the granddaughter of a wealthy Barnwell District planter, George W. Muse.

13 At home—this promises to be a wet day—we have already had one good shower before breakfast. Bottles. Joe has taken out two dozen bottles & I will strain my Old wine & put it into the new bottles.

Monday 13 Now past 12 M[id] Day. I have examined my last summer's wine— I find only sixteen bottles in the house closet good— one gal & five bottels have turned to fine vinegar. 5 bottels & one galon of last summer's wine turns out to be good vinegar—5 bottles of O[ld] Black B., good wine. 16 bottles of O[ld] Grape Do-Do. These I put in the cupboard on the 16th. 7 bottles of new B.B.—in the stair case closet. 5 Five galon keg nearly filled with new Madiera juice—small kind 1 one gal. Demijon of the same make, this I threw a few lumps of sugar into. 1 gal. of wine in Demijon.

Monday 13 in the afternoon my Old Friend Mrs. Jones came to see me[9]—we had considerable rain to day—twice the clouds were very black & angry previous to the two heavy showers.

14 Tuesday boiled the hoc half of the Old Ham that was brought out by the *wagon*. Cloudy & cool—no rain— Mrs. Jones still with me.

15 Wednesday still cool & cloudy— Mrs. Jones left me this morning— I gave Mrs. Jones one Can of Tomattos for soup—two bottels of fresh Cider, one of grape wine made in 59. This morning I put up five & a half gals. of grape juice bland Madiera.

16 Thursday After several (three) cloudy days we have a cool—beautiful bright morning—cool enough for fire. I have taken three portions of Sand's Sarsaparilla[10]—two yesterday & one before I got out of bed—I feel my throat is already better—D[r] Tally's pills made it worse in some respects—but the gargle did relieve it to some extent—yesterday heated my plums & peaches over, to day will put them up for winter. Wine. This day put into the Cupboard twenty-nine bottels of Grape wine made in 59—there are fourteen bottels of B.B. wine in

9. Seventy-nine-year-old Jane S. Jones, mother of Mrs. James Hopkins Adams and mistress of thirty-six slaves in 1860, was a well-to-do planter. In 1860 her household consisted of four young people named Scott— Pauline (fifteen), Laura (fourteen), Belton (eight), and James (six), probably her grandchildren. Born Jane Ross, she first was married to Samuel Scott, who died in 1818, and then to Darling Jones.

10. During these months, P. G. McGregor's Drug & Chemical Store in Columbia was proclaiming the merits of this New York City product— "The Greatest American Remedy for Purifying the Blood."

the same cupboard. Also put away—seven vessels with wild plum preserved last week & three of cut peaches. 16 bottles of wine I had in the house put with 13 in the cupboard made the 29—

Friday 17th I sent yesterday for D[r] Huo to meet me at Cabin branch to day[11]—he did so, we met at the gate—he from Col——— I from the sand Hills— He thinks my throat a more serious case than D[r] Tally did & I know from my own observations that D[r] Huo understands the case better than D[r] Tally did. After seeing the D[r] I went to my mill place—returned to the Sand Hills—got home about sun down. This was a fine day—not so pleasant as yesterday—a warm day—

Saturday 18 This is a bright pleasant morning— My sand Hill fodder was taken off yesterday—to day I expect the wagons from the plantation to bring it to the house. Fanny Hopkins sent yesterday while I was away to know how I was.[12]

Sunday 19 A bright day—at home, not much good feeling in me to day—Hagar—driver Sam—Maria & Mack came from the plantation.

Monday 20th A bright morning— I have botteled off one jug of B.B. wine made in 59—put a little nice brown sugar in each bottle— marked thus B.B. 1 / 14 bottles made in 59, no. in rotation—I don't think this very strong. Nectrine Seed. The long row of seed planted above the Artichokes begining East–first peaches, then cling nectrines–then the little round dark nectrines, free-stones–then the light coloured variety free stones. The row above all free stone peaches, a good quality—different kind.

Monday 20th This afternoon Kate—Laura—Ellen—Caroline & little Janie road to see me—the clouds were looming up before they got here—very soon 'twas lightning & thundering, some rain but the huge cloud gathered as it wended its way south— there was an interval & they left— I hope ere this are safe at home—Now after dark & the rain falls gently. Emma sent for figs to day by Archer. Heard Ada had a son, name

11. French-born Louis V. Huot, age twenty-nine, was associated with Dr. Samuel Fair. Their offices at Plain [Hampton] and Sumter streets included a dispensary or clinic with "accommodations" for surgical and medical patients, which sometimes included Brevard slaves.
12. Keziah also refers to Fanny, the former Frances Martha Tucker and mistress of Magnolia, as Mrs. F. M. Hopkins.

Thomas Hopkins.[13] May God watch over this child & make him a good man.

21 Tuesday I went to Emma's—had a little rain late in the afternoon.

22 Came home in the morning—Amy G. came with me, in the afternoon we rode around Adison's[14]— A——— went to the spring.

23 Thursday Amy & Laura with me[15]—had the ham boiled that came out last—by Dick—after 5 A.M. a few drops of rain. ('Twas boiled yesterday 23rd / 60 August.)

Friday 24th Amy & Laura with me—this is a bright day—Mary made me some bad looking jelly to day. Wine. Muscadine Wine. Mash the muscadines, let them stand 24 hours in a vessel, strain off the juice & let it stand 12 hours— To one gal. of juice add 2 lb. of sugar & one gill of brandy[16]—after three or four weeks bottle it— I would say—three months. Kate's receipt. I had thirty two bottles of Old wine put into the Wine cupboard on friday morning the 24th of August 1860—this makes sixty one in all—all these, I think, is wine made in 59. Sometimes I spell bottel—sometimes bottle— I think I had better consult Noah Webster— Sept. 18th This day 26 bottels of grape juice under the stair case made this year in new bottles with new juice. These made in 1860—

September 25th This day filled nine bottles with the juice of the bullace & four with wild Hog plum juice.[17] I have three bottles of the juice of the Bland Madiera in my closet (my room).

25 Emma & Sally joined us for dinner. Fanny Hopkins came after dinner & took tea—they all left this afternoon—a clear warm day this.

26 Clear—I at home alone.

---

13. Ada (Adeline Rembert) was the wife of David Hopkins (1838–1895), eldest surviving son of William and Emma Hopkins. A letter reproduced in *Lower Richland Planters* indicates that William at first objected to David's marriage, believing the couple too young to take on such responsibilities.

14. Amy Goodwyn Hopkins (1845–1896), daughter of William and Emma Hopkins. "Adison's" is a reference to Addison's Field and Addison's Spring, headwaters of Tom's Creek and what once had been the focal point of the summer village known as Adams Hill.

15. Amy Goodwyn Hopkins and Laura Keziah Adams (1843–1866).

16. A gill, pronounced "jill," equals one-fourth of a pint.

17. Bullace is a small wild or semi-domesticated plum much like the damson, but inferior. Hog plum is a yellow fruit much favored by hogs, hence the name.

27 A bright morning this—Had a bag of second quality *Flour* opened this morning of the first grinding from Green's Mill.[18] 88 lb. bag 2nd quality—now I will see how long this bag will last me. KGHB August 27th—Last night I dreamed James H. Adams & family had returned, all well— I only hope they may:—(not careing how they value me)— but for their *own* & their family's blessings I hope they may all & every one of them be blessed here & here after. My throat may be better—still it is difficult to know—some hours it seems better, then it will swell rapidly & this is the way it has been & continues to be— Oh if Jesus would take me to his own— I ought to desire to leave this world— yet a christian would not say this—we should patiently wait the will of our *Master*— Oh God make me resigned to thy dispensations— Amy Adams came unexpectedly & spent the day with me[19]—boiled the Ham that was brought out Tuesday morning. I don't think it was good. I gave A— some plums & figs to make into preserves. 'Tis now sun down.

Tuesday 28th Went to Cabin branch—saw Dr Huo—he cauterized my throat, this is the third time—some better than it was— went to Emma's at night—called again on Wednesday to order some things for Thursday's dinner.

Wednesday 29 Home to dinner—

30 Thursday This day Mrs. F. M. Hopkins—her two daughter in laws, Octavia & Anne—with their six children—Mrs. Ray with her three little girls & the babe dined with me[20]— Had a Ham—boiled & roast mutton—two fowls & vegetables for dinner—all done up in the worst order—the soup passable— I am mortified every time I have a dining— They left

---

18. This lumber/grist mill, owned by Dr. Fred Green, was located in Columbia near the bridge spanning the Congaree River.

19. Amy Goodwyn Adams (1818–1895), at this time unmarried, was the daughter of Mary and Joel Adams, Jr. She subsequently became the second wife of her first cousin, John Pickett Adams.

20. Octavia, John's wife, was the daughter of John and Maria Chappell; Anne, daughter of Edward and Claudia Houstoun, was the second wife of Fanny's other son, James. Sally Ray's three girls, ages nine to four, were named Fannie, Sally, and Mary. The "babe" was Archibald Wadsworth Ray, born 23 July 1860.

in the afternoon to attend singing at Mrs. Joel Adams, Senior.[21]

31 Friday This is the last day of this month—it is a bright pleasant day—I was not well all the morning—head ache & throat feeling unpleasant. Now just after dark & the rain is dropping a little—we need rain— I do hope it will rain this night to do some good. Quite a company I understand at Mr. Hankle's this evening[22]— I hope they may enjoy themselves & all get home safe—should the pastor of a church keep irregular hours— Fanny tells me they meet at six & 7 O'clock P.M.— & enjoy themselves till after 12 O'clock—*in truth she said* till nearly day. These were her words yesterday:—with all this they may be *far nearer Heaven* than *I am*—our works & penances will do nothing unless God justifies us. Oh my God fit me for Heaven & Lord save my dear Country—first draw all to thee— Let me *never* dare blame God for any of our troubles—he has given us light—& we choose darkness & can a Holy God tolerate the latter—very little rain fell to day, all is now still.

---

21. This apparently was the mother of Amy Goodwyn Adams, although her father (who died in 1859) was known throughout his lifetime as "Junior."

22. William Henry Hanckel was the first full-time rector of St. John's Congaree Episcopal Church, serving at that post from 1859 to 1871. During the first year of its existence (1858), St. John's was associated with Zion Episcopal Church in the eastern part of Lower Richland.

September
"These are perilous times."

1st day of
September
Saturday Randolph—his wife Kate—Laura—Ellen—Caroline & little Janie spent this afternoon with me— All of us walked out— some gathering grapes—some for pleasure— I do feel for these children when I think what a change may come over them— Their Dear father may not be spared to them long— God has promised to be a father to the Orphan—may they all turn to him in time to meet such a change.

2nd At home, not spending the day as my heart desires to spend it, my thoughts too much with the world. Lord help me!!!

3 Monday This day has been cloudy—no rain— Had wild grapes gathered to make into wine.

4 Went to Emma's, staid all night. The next morning 5th, Dr Huo came down to cauterize my throat— I [spent] some time at Cabin branch, after dinner returned to Emma's, staid all night again—

6 Thursday I came by James H. Adams' & got home in the afternoon[1]—

7 Friday had my wild grapes strained, made seven bottles of the juice—put into the stair case closet this morning, the 8th Saturday—the 7 bottles of Wild grape & seven of the Bland Madiera— We have not yet had rain sufficient to sow my main crop of turnips— This is a pleasant day in the house, but the sun shines *hot*— I wish I had a thermometer. Sometimes I feel so thankful to know I can sit & read when I please—reading is my greatest happiness of late— Oh God I thank thee for this feeling—let me never cease to be thankful for *the least* privilege to do right—& Oh keep down all sinful risings in this breast of mine—for they are many—*Satan never sleeps,* he is near at all hours, light & darkness are the same to him—ever striving to draw us from *God*— Lord, Lord—save us—save our *dear dear Country first.* These are perilous times—perilous because we do not love God as we should—often do we read in his Holy word of his suffering

---

1. The Adams home, Live Oak, was about a mile from Congaree, land now in McEntire Air Base.

nations to overcome nations for their sins—so soon as they turn to him in sincerity & truth, he is merciful.

9th Sunday A beautiful pleasant morning—out doors the sun is very warm—but the breeze is pleasant. I don't know what is to become of me— I neglect attending church so often I feel very bad about it, I confess I am wrong in neglecting this duty, 'tis my business to honour God's appointments & I do pray to have it in my power to be more devoted to his cause— Lord thou canst order all things for my good—help me to devote *my all to thee*—for whom have I on earth to look to but *thee—thou great eternal.*

> "Blessed is the man that keepeth the sabbath
> from polluting it, & keepeth his hands from
> doing any evil." v. LVI. Isaiah.

Monday 10th This is a cloudy morning—last evening, rather in the afternoon, we had a nice drizzle of rain. This day weighed the wool I wish to send to the factory[2]—eighty nine lb. with four sacks it is in—as follows—one sack 18¼—21—25¾—25¼ gross.

11 Tuesday I went to my mill place—took Mary—Ned—Tom—Dorcas—Jim & John—servants to do service. Emma Hopkins, her son James—daughters Amy & Sally joined me—we hoped to have a fish dinner but the cloudy morning detained us too late to get fish— We had enough for a taste of fish, plenty of ham & fried fowl, 'twas the first dinner in my new Old house[3]—went & slept at Cabin branch.

12th Wednesday Went to Col., made my purchases for fall and winter—

13 in the street again & I hope I will not be obliged to go to Col. again soon as I have got a supply of winter clothing for negroes.[4] Met my Sister in Col., *poor dear Sister,* your life has been throughout more like a stream flowing over shoal after shoal than any thing else—scar[c]e a smooth current in its

---

2. This was the well-known Saluda Factory located just west of Columbia in Lexington District.

3. Keziah had hired Tom Prescott to make repairs at this site, hence the words "my new Old house." Her domestic notes reveal this work included a new kitchen, which cost $40: "I now wish I had never thought of building it . . . I get money it all goes faster than it was made."

4. In mid-nineteenth-century jargon, "in the street" meant shopping in Columbia's business district—"going downtown."

whole course— Oh that God would make your entrance into another life very different.

Thursday 13 I purchased crockery—from Mr. Stanley for my mill Home[5]—at night at Emma's—

Friday 14 This morning I got home to my Sand Hill residence having been absent since tuesday morning—fine pleasant weather— all the time rather cool in the mornings—this the coolest morn we have had. I came home with—65 Dollars in paper, 3 Dollars & 10 cts. in Silver. Took 300 to pay bills &c., &c.—the 69 all that is left. Heard Mrs. Jones—Kate & Laura called yesterday evening. Truely sorry they came while I was absent, for I love to see them all. Have given Joe two dozen wine bottels to clean—these for Bullace & Shupernong.

15th Saturday I went to Cabin Branch place to day to get my jelly glasses, brought out one doz. plates—two large water pitchers, one doz. & nine glasses for putting up jelly—Three night mugs [chamber pots]—One doz. white cups & saucers—these I expect to keep in the Sand Hills. This morning was cloudy, some appearance of rain through the day—but not a drop fell. Sister sent for help to have a beef killed— I sent Harry & Joe—she sent me some nice beef in return— Oh what a life of anxiety we all live. 'tis said a christian should ever be cheerful & happy— I am all the time sad—sometimes apparently happy— I think I seldom feel very happy— Lord make me more useful in thy cause— My heart has grown cold in religious duties—help me to feel a deeper interest in every thing that *my* Master commands I should— Oh make me thine—wholy thine, *Oh my God*. This night, if reports are true, had been set apart to cut us off— Oh God, because we own slaves— Lord thou knowest our hearts—save us for a calmer end & let us never cease to think & to bless thee for thy loving kindness— Lord, save this our good country & make us *all* & *every one*, bond & free, to love thee & do thy will as good servants—*we* are *all* thy servants—all in thy hands—Oh save us.

16th Sept. At home—Mack—Maria—little John & little William out to *1860* day.

---

5. William B. Stanley operated a china emporium at 170 Richardson [Main] Street.

Monday 17th This is a cloudy morning— I do hope we may have rain to day. I have given Joe two dozen bottels to clean. Bottels. X

18 We had a little rain yesterday—more cloud than rain—as little as it was I concluded to sow the late turnip seed—a few beet seed mixed with them & I have commenced ploughing in rye. Cloudy to day—only one drizzle so far. I have Mary making jelly from the N.C. greening[6]—

18 Joe found only 12 bottels. Jelly— Made four lb. of sugar into apply jelly—filled five glass pt. jars—not very stiff. This is 19th Wednesday— Now past 12 M[id] day—looks like clearing off— Oh my God I have so many little things to unnerve me— I wish I was prepared to die & could go to my God. I wish to be kind to my negroes—but I receive little but impudence from Rosanna & Sylvia—it is a truth if I am compelled to speak harshly to them—after bearing every thing from them I get impudence— Oh my God give me fortitude to do what is right to these then give me firmness to go no farther— At my death it is my solemn desire that Tama— Sylvia—Mack—Maria & Rosanna be sold— I cannot think of imposing such servants on any one of my heirs.

Thursday Last evening we had a pouring rain— I fear it has buried my
20th/60 turnip seed so deep they can never get up. This is a pretty morning bright & placid looking—not too warm yet— I think 'twill be warm by 12 o'clock. Heard last night that James H. Adams got home—wife & daughter with him[7]— I am thankful he has been spared to his dear family—do hope he may be a useful man to his country & a good man to his family as long as he lives. J. H. A.———— has left his son Warren in Europe[8]— J. H. A. got home on Wednesday the 19th of September 1860. This morning James Hopkins & his wife Anne called to see me & asked me to go over tomorrow evening & see them for the last visit— They leave in a few days for Florida.

---

6. Greening is a term for several varieties of green-skinned apples.

7. Jane Margaret Scott Adams and their eldest unmarried daughter, Jane Margaret (1841–1911), who subsequently married (1) States Rights Gist and (2) John Hampden Brooks. The purpose of this trip had been to consult European specialists concerning the health of Adams, who was suffering from cancer.

8. Warren (1838–1880) later married Nathalie Heyward, daughter of Nathaniel and Eliza Barnwell Smith Heyward.

Friday 21st I went to my mill place—stoped at Cabin branch on my return—changed my riding dress for a black silk dress & went on to Mrs. F. M. Hopkins where I found quite an assembling of the neighbours met to sing, dance & pass off the evening—all went pleasantly— I ended this day by spending the night at J. H. A———— J. H. A. has fattened—he brought me a pretty present of a small mantle ornament— Jane his wife brought me a very pretty little box of Swiss work from Geneva.[9] Fine weather.

Saturday 22 Got home between one & two O'clock A.M.—called to Sister—found her up—complaining of debility. Fine day. Now after supper— I have put up four bottels of the juice of the wild plum today. Yesterday Mary spoiled six lb. of loaf sugar in failing to make jelly.

23 Sunday at home—servants—Nelly, Dave & Tama—here—a fine day, had a fowl cooked for dinner & the last Ham boiled—

24th I sent by Jim for another ham today—he has gone down to have my horses shod. This is Monday the 24th—a beautiful morning—thus Sylvia washing—Dick has four blankets to wash—24th of Sept., Jim got home late & brought the ham. Had two loaves of bread made to day.

25th This is a beautiful morning, I am feeling very badly. I have just been to the store room & counted the bottels of grape juice put away in Mr. Adams' cupboard, precisely one hundred & three bottels including the black berry & two one gal. demijohns— I very much fear it will turn out vinegar instead of wine, all these in one cupboard, I am so forgetful— I am obliged to be minute— I will now go & count the bottels I have in the house—there is no more fruit to convert into wine. I have counted these & have in the closets in my house—fifty bottels, 3 three large demijohns one gal. each—one three gal. jug & one two gal. jug—part of this made in 1859 & some in 1860, all the bottels are labelled— I also have three kegs nearly filled with grape juice— I think about ten gallons in the three kegs—this I will put into bottels after awhile—this estimate is correct as possible—no exaggeration about it. 25th. day of Sept. 1860—KGHB, according to my estimate I ought to have forty gallons making either wine or vinegar—'twill take time to test it,

---

9. Probably a box of lace.

KGHB. I forgot some [of] the jugs— I think it should be forty five gallons—KGHB. On the evening of the 25th my friend Mrs. Jones came to see me.

26th Wednesday I sent my carriage for Mary Brooks & Laura—Mary brought her babe P. with her—they returned in the afternoon.[10] I sent J. H. A. some cider.

27th Mrs. Jones left me after breakfast.

28 I went to Cabin branch & examined my hams—out of 68—I found 11 (eleven) bad ones, the balance very good. I have ordered 7 good ones brought out on Monday, hung the balance of the good ones to themselves 50 & the bad ones together. Went in the evening to E. & this morning 29th came back home to the Sand Hills. This morning I paid Wm Hopkins by check all I owed him for land—took up his note of 820 & some cts.[11] Now only one debt to man hangs over me.

30th Sept. the last day of this month— I have been to church to day— Oh God I thank thee that thou didst help me to this act— feeble as it is—it thus gives me better feelings & Oh how thankful I am for the help—a little cloudy today.

---

10. Mary Goodwyn Adams (1836–1866), eldest daughter of James Hopkins Adams, was the first wife of John Hampden Brooks. The "babe" was Preston Brooks II, born 6 January 1860. Following Mary's death, Brooks married her younger sister, Jane, widow of General States Rights Gist.

11. This transaction involved the purchase in the late 1850s of a small piece of land, 39¾ acres.

October
"Oh My God save this Country!!!"

Oct. 1st A pleasant day—cloudy in the afternoon. Tasted some of my juice of the grape to day with Mary A. Kitterson[1]—thought it tasted like wine. Harrison is quite sick to day—put a blister on him by Dr Ray's advice, poor little fellow, I wish he could get well.[2]

Oct. 2nd Making preparations to go to Col.— I mislaid two keys—some little drizling of rain to day— I am now undecided whether to go to Col. or not. Having tomattos prepared for cans. Soup Tomattos.

Oct. 2 At home, cloudy day—

Oct. 3 Left home early in the morning—cloudy— I had promised to meet some friends in Columbia—felt bound to go. The rain commenced before I descended the high hill at little creek branch—& it really poured until we reached Hampton's Old field—got to Col. at eleven O'clock.

4th Thursday still in Col. & a very wet day—

5th I gladly left Columbia— I never spent many nights as lonely as these two were spent— I sacrificed feelings to go & accommodate friends & lo not one met me there— Oh I felt sad, very sad—ten times more so at night than in the day— Oh my God fit me for Heaven & take me from this boisterous land—where is our happiness—can we anticipate any thing but storms from man—no—no—but God can stay the hand of the assasin. I staid at Emma's last night—saw Cousin Ada & her boy—he is a fine looking little Thomas.

6th Came home this morning— Mrs. Deas & Miss Septima Chappell stoped at my door on their way to Mr. Hanckle's.[3]

---

1. The seventeen-year-old daughter of neighbor Richard Kitterson.
2. Keziah perhaps had applied a mustard plaster or something of that sort to the chest of this critically ill youngster, son of one of her slaves.
3. Mrs. Marion Deas (age thirty-five) and Septima (thirty), sisters of Paul H. Chappell (thirty-nine), a planter whose lands were adjacent to those of Keziah.

They are to spend Tuesday the 9th with me— I hope I may be well enough to enjoy their company. I took a ham to Col.—brought it back home whole.

7th Sunday I have spent a part of this morning reading my bible and some of Dr Scott's letters[4] & I confess as anxious as I am to do the will of my Master Jesus, I found myself nodding, proving there is the same nature in me that those had who slept while Jesus was praying. The skies are much clearer in the E. to day than they are in the West—no rain, not much sunshine.

Monday 8th At home, a fine day— I made cake—total failure in the baking—

Tuesday 9th My Company came—dined with me & I hope they spent the day pleasantly— Mrs. F. M. Hopkins & her two grand children (son James' children), Mrs. Deas, her little son John—Miss Septima chappell & they brought their little niece Fanny Hopkins—Mrs. Jane M. Adams— My niece Janie, Laura & Carry— They are now I hope all safe at their respective homes—by this time 7 O'clock A.M.[5] We walked out after dinner & all seemed happy— I had for dinner one of the seven hams which were hung to the left, & brought out to the Sand Hills—one Old Gobbler—pig & chickens— we also had milk & peaches this 9th day of Oct. 1860.

Oct. 10th This is a fine day— I have enjoyed out door work this morning, now 12 O'clock. Another day now ended. Oh my Master what have I done for thee? nothing—nothing, but I have been zealous for self— Lord forgive me—& make me to think more of my God. Ned & Dick gone home tonight to stay T. F. & Saturday to pick cotton, it seems to me I miss them & really do not like to make them do such hard work— they are house boys & cannot stand the sun as the field hands do.

Oct. 11th This is a hazy day— I have been busy all day—my shoulder pained me all the time— I really know not what to think of this poor right shoulder—'tis now near three months since

4. Dr. W. A. Scott, editor of San Francisco's *Pacific Expositor*, a well-known Presbyterian clergyman.

5. Keziah probably means P.M. James's two children were David Thomas (1852–1869) and Frances Tucker (born September 1853). "Little niece Fanny" is his brother John's daughter (1854–1894), who strangely also was named Frances Tucker Hopkins.

my throat was first sore—not well yet & my shoulder no better than it has been. The D[r] says it is nervous rheumatism. I am sure I cannot say— Poor little Harrison, he is swolen under the eyes—poor child I know not what would be best for for him— The D[r] has given him medicine lately, it does him no good that I can see. I must try the jerusalem seed[6]— Oh if I could only take time & give him more attention. I wish he would be spared for his parents but Lord thou knowest best what to do & let me not ask too fervently for his recovery. Jim finished ploughing rye in the Old garden today, this 11th of Oct.

12th This morning was cloudy—this afternoon it changed to quite a cool evening. I went to the plantation to day, received a letter from Goodwyn Ross— I wrote to Mr. J. A. Crawford on business.[7] Since I took coffee I have answered Goodwyn's letter—left out a jar of three gallons of lard & two hams to be sent to Miss Lucy & Miss Polly Hays, a present for those worthy girls[8]—the Lord provide for them in my prayer. Oh My God save this Country!!! Miss Richburg at the plantation sewing for Sarah Rawlinson— Sarah is to be one of Margaret Haley's bridesmaids.[9] Heard from Mary A. Kitterson this morning before I left—no better, sent her three lemons—all I had.

13th Saturday This is a cold cloudy morning. Kitterson has sent word he would kill a beef to day, I am to take a part of it. I wonder how those who held torches last night feel this morning— some heavy heads I guess[10]—it is time for us to shew the

---

6. Seeds of the Jerusalem artichoke, a sunflower-like weed.

7. Jesse Goodwyn Ross, eldest grandson of Keziah's half-brother, Jesse Howell Goodwyn, was attending the University of North Carolina and would be her house guest during the Christmas season. J. A. Crawford, president of Columbia's Commercial Bank, was the man who sold Keziah her city property in 1847.

8. Lucy and Polly (ages sixty and sixty-five respectively) were maiden ladies living in Lower Richland.

9. One of the Rawlinson children married a Richbourg, hence the connection to that local family. Sixteen-year-old Margaret Haley, whose parents had moved to Texas, was living in the household of Charles Roach in 1860. The departure of Matthew Haley elicited this comment from diarist Samuel Leland: "He was an Irishman and a Catholic— ergo—let him go."

10. A reference to a political rally held in Columbia during the 1860 presidential campaign.

rabble of the North we are not to be murdered in cold blood because we own slaves—there are no doubts but thousands would have prefered being born in this beautiful country without the encumbrance—but they have been transmitted down to us & what we can do with them?—free such a multitude of half barbarians in our midst—no—no—we must sooner give up our lives than submit to such a degredation— From the time I could reason with myself I wished there was a way to get rid of them—but not free them in our midst yet. They are not prepared for freedom, many of them set no higher value on themselves than the beasts of the field do— I know a family in five miles of me where there are six women who have & have had children for thirty years back & not one of them but have [been] bastards & only one ever had a husband. There are many who have some pride of character & perhaps some would do a little better if they had religion set before them in its true colours—but when it is known & seen that the whites act as real infidels fearless of any power, we can pity the ignorant—but none of them are so ignorant as not to be accountable to God—they all have & have had gospel privileges for generations back—they are prone as human nature ever is to do evil—& instead of striving against it—yield to it—of course we must make allowance for their ignorance & this is the only paleative. That wretch John Brown—if he had come as one of christ's Apostles & preached down sin he might have been the instrument of good—but he come to cut our throats because we held property we could not do otherwise with—was preposterous— Did God set the children of Israel to cutting their masters' throats to flee [free] them from bondage— no—no—he brought them out of Egypt in his own peculiar way & he can send Africa's sons & daughters back when he knows they are ready for their exode. I own many slaves & many of the females are of the lowest cast—making miserable their own fellow servants by medling with the husbands of others— I am not excusing the males, but in the world they are not so degraded by such conduct as the females— but *I do hope & pray* that every one will be made to suffer here on this earth, who mars the peace of another— This is a dirty subject—& had I not thought of those cruel abolitionists who wish to free such people in our midst I would not have spoken this truth here— God is good— Lord Jesus save us from degredation—let us draw *nearer & nearer to all that is beautiful & good in thy sight.*

14th Sunday A cloudy cold blowing day—so cloudy early I had no thought of going to church—this day Mr. Beverly expects to collect to take to the associations[11]— I sent him ten dollars enclosed by Jim— I desire my mite to be appropriated to the education of young men for the ministry & yet I know not whether it will do much good— I may judge others by my-self—it seems to me there is very little godliness in the world—there is nothing but strife—ambition goes a head of every thing & that [is] not a laudable ambition—every one seeks *his own* & *his own immediate family's* agrandisement—it seems to me our dear Country is to be sacrificed to selfish notions. 12 O'clock—still cloudy & windy— This day drags heavily with me— Lord help me to enjoy it more— Another sabbath ended— I have been reading the book of Jeremiah to day as far as the 9th chapter— Oh God it makes my heart sad to read of such sorrowful scenes— Why is it that man has been prone from the beginning to follow every sin in dis-obedience to the commands of *God?*—why not love the things that are *good* & hate *vice*? Oh my God this is one thing I cannot see into—follow sin in prefference to trying to keep God's commands—is there any thing more difficult in doing right than wrong?—no Lord Jesus thy ways are lovely but man, in a natural state, *is a poor miserable erring creature*—an empty earthen vessel—no "treasures therein"—Lord Jesus I feel I have not spent this day as I desire to do so—my thoughts, if any, not seriously disposed— Help me, Oh my master, to be a better servant & prepare me for death— This Lord is my sincere prayer to keep in my mind—life is short & not put off for tomorrow what I can do to day for my soul's salvation. Lord remember me & make me thine—wholy thine—& Oh my God take under thy special care my *poor dear lonely* sister— O God her sorrows have been long & severe—God pity her & comfort her for Jesus sake who suf-fered for us all. Lord draw reluctant hearts to thee where ever found. Make *my servants* (those who labor for me) to know thee & love thee is one of my constant prayers.

---

11. William D. Beverly (age thirty-six) was pastor of Lower Richland's Beulah Baptist Church. His family consisted of his thirty-three-year-old wife, Rachel, and three children.

15th I went home & gave out cloth at Cabin branch to most of the men & women.

16 Came home this morning—called to see Mrs. Hammond[12] on my way home, yesterday was cold—this is a fine bright day. I hear so much of this negro excitement I fear it will make me callous instead of bitter—but I will pray for a preparation for a better home.

17th Wednesday at home—had Light bread & quince Marmalade made— The wagon came out to day & hauled in five loads of corn.

18 Still gathering in corn— This is a very fine bright day. Mrs. Dick Adams sent 2 Doz. eggs to exchange for lard[13]— I sent her 2 lb. To day I weighed seven egg[s] that weighed 14 oz.— Making cake, expecting Mrs. R[awlinson] & Miss R[ichbourg] to dine with me—poor me—poor me—

18th At night — Gathered in nine wagon loads of corn from the large field— I think it yielded well— I hope to make one load & a half from my late corn. Next year I must try to make more corn out there— I have a great many to provide for & I wish to treat them well & teach them how to improve themselves. My horses missing this evening— Jim has gone for them, he should have a pass[14]— I fear he will be taken up. I know I neglect visiting sister— Lord my Master, if the prayers of one can help another, assist me to pray for my Dear Sister & all my Dear relatives— Oh my God save this dear Country of ours & help all thy children to all that is pleasing in thy sight. Oh God remember what poor creatures we are, both the bond & the free. Thankful I am Heavenly Father that James H. Adams seems to be better— Lord make him one of thy children & draw all his family near thee.

19th This is Friday—a boisterous morn this is— I shall not look for Mrs. R. to day unless there is a great change before 10 O'clock. Negroes such trying creatures you are— The first thing I saw like work this morning was Rosanna with a box of collards out of my garden— I have very few there, the hot

---

12. Ann C. Hammond (age thirty-nine), wife of farmer Elias Hammond.

13. Mrs. Dick Adams may have been Rebecca Adams, who is mentioned later, the young wife of a poor planter who lived nearby.

14. Theoretically slaves needed passes or "papers" when traveling about the countryside unaccompanied by whites. Without a pass, they might be seized by patrols organized for the purpose of apprehending runaways and suppressing unlawful activity.

summer prevented my saving but very few. I have a plenty of turnips, gave them as many as they wanted yesterday & the day before & intended they should have [more] when they wished. I make John stay in the Kitchen in wet weather & try to keep her [Rosanna] out of the rain—but she could leave my breakfast & go through the rain to deceive me. Oh I wish I had been born in a Christian land & never seen or known of slaves of any colour. A degraded population is a curse to a country. Negroes are as deceitful & lying as any people can well be— Lord give me better feelings towards them. (Forgive me Lord, for unkind thoughts & have mercy on me!)

Saturday 20th This day cloudy— I went to E. late in the afternoon— To day sent Sister some Turkey & jelly— Oh my Father pity the desolate—watch over us though we are unworthy.

Sunday 21 At Emma's all day—this a good day—but cool— I sent a servant to Mr. Paul Chappell's with a note for O. H.—when I do these little things (in the eyes of the world) I feel I am disobeying God's commands[15]— Oh my Father make me to serve thee better & Oh how thankful I am that thou has drawn me from the world to some degree— Oh fit me for Heaven & do not leave me to see & know the troubles that are comeing upon us— Lord shall I distrust thee? "Behold he that keepeth Israel shall neither slumber nor sleep." This is comforting— Oh that we were a people who followed Christ more closely. "As the mountains are round about Jerusalem, so the Lord is round about his people henceforth, even forever"—here is comfort, let us never doubt God's goodness. This night some of my friends are in Col— God Almighty!! be with them—be with us who are scattered through the land & save us from our enemies—thou hast said, "The rod of the wicked shall not rest upon the lot of the righteous, lest the righteous put forth their hands into iniquity."— Oh suffer none of thy servants to disobey thee nor to stray from thee.

22 Monday I left Emma's this morning—called at J. H. Adams', met my friend Mrs. Jones there— I had heard that my nephew was looking well— I was sadly disappointed, poor man, he

---

15. O. H. was Octavia Chappell Hopkins, Paul's sister and wife of John Hopkins. Just why Keziah thought she was "disobeying God's commands" is unclear.

is looking very badly & was very low spirited— I do feel very much for him— Lord make him thine, wholy thine, is my prayer—do I sin when I dwell on troubles attending us while on earth— My Master thou hast made all things good & beautiful—but wicked man seems determined to destroy the peace of his brother man— Oh save us— Oh save us from the power of man. Now near nine O'clock at night & I am at home in the Sand Hills at Mt. Ed as I sometimes call this place—sometimes I call it the very reverse, Mt. Trouble. This has been a fine day—called at Sister['s], she had gone to Columbia. Oh that my Master would claim her & all of us as his own. This day I heard that poor Sally Doby (that was) is a great sufferer, she will be far better off with God than we who are left in this world of trials[16]— Oh that I was near my Master.

Tuesday morning 23rd This is as lovely a morn as ever shone— Can it be that God will set any one over us who is not worthy to rule this beautiful Country— Lord, if thou dost this thing, it is because we deserve it—save our Country, Oh My God. Mrs. Rawlinson & Miss Richburg dined with me to day— Turkey—ham & fowl for dinner.

Wednesday 24th This is another beautiful morn—every thing to invite man to purity—but I fear there are very few who think for themselves in these exciting times— God does punish his people for sinning against his commands—& have we not as a people made riches our God— I feel it is ever a sin with me—& I know I do not dwell on these things as I have known others to do— "Judge not lest ye be judged" I add here—for I know my trespasses are mountain high, but I do try to avoid commiting those sins God plainly forbids—anger & unpleasant thoughts often rise in this breast of mine—but all that is filthy I immediatley call on God to help me put down— I do hate mean thoughts as well as bad acts— *I do abhor sins of low degree.* Lord God—Almighty!! Save this our *dear—dear country* & pity thy poor unworthy servants—they know not how good thou has been to them—& those Northern cut throats— Oh Change their wicked hearts—they know no God or they never could have the feelings they have towards us— I must now stop or give way to feelings I should not—

16. Sarah English Doby (born 1838), wife of Alfred Brevard of Camden, a cousin of Keziah's late husband.

how can a southerner love those whose highest glory would be to know we were exterminated to give place to a people far inferior— I wish every vessel that would go to Africa to bring slaves here—could sink before they reached her soil.[17] I would give up every ct. I own on earth if it could stop the slave trade— My reason is this—we have a hard time with them & I feel for those who are to come after us. We never would have been unhappy with slaves if white people had been true to their white brethern & our Negroes would now have been happy if all & every one had made the religion of christ their *North Star*—but religion is in shew—vanity & shew, Man's God. I too have yielded a shade to the sins that beset us— Lord help me?—

Thursday 25th Still beautiful out doors—the atmosphere has asumed a muddy appearance at a distance—which from my observation points to bad weather brewing—too warm to day to be pleasant— I suffered a good deal last night with my shoulder—my throat was sore this morning—better now at 12 O'clock. I wish I could spend more time in doing good to others.

Friday 26th This is a pretty day—something like the Indian summer day.

27th Saturday A pretty morning— I suffered very much last night from my arm & early this morning sent for Dr Ray— I am expecting him every minute— This is a singular shoulder— I suffer at night more than I do in the day. What are my thoughts this morning—not in a good frame of mind— Lord make me better— My desire is to live to thee—to try to be fit to sit at thy feet when it pleases thee to take me to my eternal home—all my time do I long to devote to thee. At night Dr Ray came & pronounced my case just what Dr Hugho did— Neuralgia of the shoulder— I fear they are only right in part— Mine is not a common sore throat & time I fear will shew it— My System is diseased & has been ever since I was vaxinated from Sally Hopkins' arm when she was not more than six or seven years old—all of us who were vaxinated then had dreadful arms—the matter must

17. Of course, any such traffic was illegal in 1860, although, ironically, Keziah's nephew, James Hopkins Adams, was among those who in the 1850s advocated reopening this trade.

have been impure. Judge L[ongstreet's] Georgia scenes are near—sometimes I laugh over them until I cry—at this moment I feel no desire to open them[18]—

28 Sunday This has been a cloudy day—the clouds were very changeable, sometimes very dark in the W., sometimes very dark in the N., S. & E., the brisk breeze made them flighty indeed— I thought this morning I would spend the day better than I have—but Lord, what can frail human do without thee? it is now night & I feel I have spent this day idly, no good thing have I done—neither have I committed a willing sin—but Oh I have been cold & indifferent in every act— My God I *plead* for help from thee— I am almost heartless at times—this is when I think of the state of our *dear—dear Country*— Lord save it—& chastise thy rebellious children in some other way than that of putting us in the power of man— Unregenerate unenlightened man is the most terrific animal on earth— Jesus Master come to our assistance & change the hearts of those whose desire seems to be to exterminate us in the most horid manner— Oh my God—my religion as weak as it [is, is] my only comfort in these stirring times— Oh Heavenly Father save my country & have mercy on thy unworthy servants—let not the horrors of India be acted here on American soil—the soil that has been hailed as the refuge of the oppressed of other lands— My God my prayer is first for my Country—then Lord prepare me for a better world & take me—my negroes will not need me— thou canst bless them after taking us all from this world— I have had many crosses from some few & thought them dreadful trials—but they were drops in the bucket compared to even the thoughts of what may come over us—yet why should my heart sink within me—when I have all the days of my life—clung to thee, though as unworthy as I am Thou has promised to hear our pleadings— Lord strengthen my faith. D[r] Scott says heartlessness is "dishonourble to the mercy & grace of the gospel, & to *his* name who commands his servants rejoice in hope." Oh God, how consoling to hear this from such a good man as D[r] Scott must have been—he

---

18. Augustus Baldwin Longstreet (1790–1870)—jurist, author, educator—became president of South Carolina College in 1857. His *Georgia Scenes*, first published in book form in 1835, had many admirers.

was a very humble christian & considered all that is not truthful & pure the veriest sin.

Monday 29th This morning a very hard & long rain—in the afternoon I went to my Cabin branch place—stoped the night.

30 gave out cloth to day—the women got wool for frocks— women, men & children—shirts & shemise—this evening late went to Emma's—staid all night—

31 Left Emma's, took Sally H[opkins] with me to my mill place—there gave out—wool to the men for coats & wool to the women for frocks—shirts & shemise to all old & young, large & small—returned to Cabin branch & stoped at night—both tuesday & wednesday had cloudy days—the afternoon brighter than the morn.

November
"This morning heard that Lincoln was elected."

Nov. 1st This is a cloudy drizly morn— I came home to the Sand Hills, brought Sally with me— This afternoon has been a bad one, very rainy— Oh God I am sad now—we have nothing before us to hope for, view our situation in any way & it seems desperate—but God can spare us— I wish I was a cheerful christian, one whose faith could carry them through. My God spare me from witnessing war & murder— *My God save our Country.*

Nov. 1st boiled half a ham today— Sally with me—had green corn for dinner. I took little Harrison with me monday—folded a coverlid [coverlet] & laid him on the front seat in my carriage—had a coverlid folded under his head—poor little fellow, I wish he could get well for his parents' comfort— No one should mourn too much for the loss of any member of their family— Oh that God had made me one of his flock & taken me long before this— My God take me quickly— Oh I fear to stay here. My god give my servants true religion. We are all to see trouble, I fear— God spare us— I expect nothing from man—all good must come from *God*—sometimes I hope our dear country is not to be torn asunder— again I see no alternative & I know there is none unless *God* says peace—be still. Oh my God save this pleasant land & make all thy creatures to bow to thee alone. (God's ways are not ours— Oh how thankful they are not.)

Nov. 2nd Last night we had great rains— I do not know when so much rain fell in one night— This is a cloudy morning—all hands in the new ground. I am very much affraid of fire— but when the fanatics of the No——— think they are doing God service to destroy us & our property, we have a great deal to keep us unhappy— I have thought so much of their course to the South—that I feel I wish my anxiety could be ended. At night— Emma has been to see me to day— I sent Harry to Mrs. D. Adams for E[mma], he got six doz. eggs at

15 cts. & Mrs. A. is to let her have 15 young hens at 15 cts. each— E. took Sally home with her—poor child she was anxious to stay a few days with me—her mother knows best & I never like to insist too much—fearing something might happen—we are not looking for— I feel I am in a responsible place when I have the care of another. My Heavenly Master pity your rebellious children— Lord we have much to contend with when we strive to subdue our sinful uprisings. Not much rain to day—a little this morning—this afternoon the sun shone out. All hands to spare burnt logs in the new ground to day— John went home with a note— Jim went home for cloth—two errands the same day to one place & still things neglected. (God's ways are not ours—bless the Lord that they are not—)

Nov. 2nd[1] This morning I went up stairs & had a bag of seconds brought down—weight 53 lb.—there are now in the L[eft] hand room fourteen bags of flour 1 [st] & 2 [nd] qualities & in the passage 2 bags of good flour & one of shorts. KGHB FLOUR above. KGHB

Sunday 4th Nov. At home—a fine bright day.

5 At home expecting Mary Brooks this afternoon. A bright day this. I was disappointed—no company. Received a letter to day from dear Harriet[2]— I always loved her—wish I could be with her for awhile.

Tuesday 6th This morning is cloudy—lent the cart to Mrs. Kitterson to day.[3] Ned gone with the wagon to Mrs. Perry's for turkeys, I am to get ten.[4] Sylvia still at the *safron* coloured curtains— Mary mending the old passage Carpet.

7th Wednesday Last night was a blowing night—this morning clear—very cold to night— I fear a frost will destroy every thing this night. Mrs. Rebecca Adams spent to day with me—let the cart to Mrs.K——— again to day—dug a few potatoes— They are so trifling I don't know that I will save any more. My Country are you safe from the spoiler? God grant that you may [y]et be spared & Oh My Heavenly Father make us all to serve thee faithfully. KGHB. Mrs. D. Adams says put

---

1. Keziah means November 3rd.
2. Harriet is subsequently identified as Harriet R. Russell of Marietta, Georgia.
3. Mary's mother, wife of neighbor Richard Kitterson.
4. Mrs. Perry, mother of a large brood, was the forty-five-year-old wife of Jesse Perry, a local farmer.

three table spoon full of slacked lime in a quart of meal for ten dung hill hens & give this quantity three times a week[5]— then rest three weeks & give again three times a week—it must be mixed in moderately warm water.

Thursday 8th This is a lovely day— I do hope no soul will intrude on me this day— I am always busy— I have little time for company & my shoulder is really painful. Dear H[arriet], tell you what I am reading— I read a little here & a little there & very little at last, my bible is my regular morning book & sometimes I forget that— I have been lately reading the life of that excellent man Dr Scott— now close to its close. I do wish I was not such a sinner—the best book cannot keep mean human nature down—anger—oh what a master you are— Oh God what would I give to conquer every sin I have— *I do hate, I do abominate sin* & yet it is in this foul frame of mine— God Almighty—help me— Oh help me to be an *humble—truthful christian.*

Friday Morning Oh My God!!! This morning heard that Lincoln was
the 9th elected— I had prayed that God would thwart his election in some way & I prayed for my *Country*— Lord we know not what is to be the result of this—but I do pray if there is to be a crisis—that we all lay down our lives sooner than free our slaves in our midst—no soul on this earth is more willing for justice than I am, but the idea of being mixed up with free blacks is *horrid*!! I must trust in God that he will not forget us as unworthy as we are— Lord save us— *I would give my life to save my Country.* I have never been opposed to giveing up slavery if we could send them out of our Country— I have often wished I had been born in just such a country—with all our religious previleges & liberties with none of them in our midst—if the North had let us alone— the Master & the servant were happy with our advantages— but we had had vile wretches ever making the restless worse than they would have been & from my experience my own negroes are as happy as I am:—happier—I never am cross to my servants without cause & they give me impudence if I find the least fault, this is of the women, the men are not half as impudent as the women are. I have left a serious & what has been an *all absorbing* theme to a common one—but

5. Dung hill chickens were common barnyard fowl fit for eating, but not for fighting and the cockpit.

the die is cast—"Caesar has past the Rubicon." We now have to act, God be with us is my prayer & let us all be willing to die rather than free our slaves in their present uncivilized state.

9th This is a cloudy, drizly day—well Abolitionists you desire our blood—*you* are not better than *we* are & God can say *to you* "this *far– & no farther*"— Mary Brooks wrote me a note this morning, from it I learnt the sad news that Lincoln was elected— This day corresponds with the note, it is so gloomy looking. Mary['s] note not gloomy—except the information about the election— Lincoln— Nature seems to be weeping o'er our cause. Late in the afternoon—still dark & rainy. I have written three letters to day—'tis now late at night & the wind is high. I will try & not be superstitious— Dr Scott had no room for such *concerts* in his great mind— "Superstition is only for fettered minds—for those who believe in man instead of God."

Saturday 10th a blowing day. I went to Cabin branch—poor little Harrison, Sam's child, died about eleven O'clock last night— he was neatly shrouded & I gave them a large sheet (No. 5) to put into the coffin—he has gone to his God, poor little Sufferer while here—now forever happy. Went to Emma's & remained the night.

11th Sunday Left E—, came to church— Mr. Beverly gave us an appropriate & excellent sermon— Substance—if judgments began at the house of God, where should the sinner appear— what would be their troubles if christians had to be chastised—came home from church. This is a bright day— quite cool.

12 Monday This morning I called to see Mrs. Ray—thence to call on Mrs. Brooks at Genl Adams'[6]— She is a pleasant lady— I think her affected in talking, perhaps it is natural—raised in a city—some who are have what we think an acquired manner— while at the Gov[ernor's]—I saw Amy Adams—Mrs. P. Chappell—Mrs. Deays—Miss Septima—my friend Mrs.Jones—Rev^d Mr. H[anckel], his wife & three nice look-

---

6. Apparently Mary Parsons Carroll Brooks (1800–1870), mother-in-law of Mary Goodwyn Adams Brooks and mother of Preston Brooks, the man who caned Senator Charles Sumner. James Hopkins Adams was called General because of his rank in the state militia as a young man.

ing children— Mrs. B[everly] was the only one who seemed to have an acquired manner—all the others were very free from it— Mrs. H. is a charleston lady yet her manners are very natural. Mrs. Jones' cap took my fancy—*& I am too old to be so foolish.* This is a fine day—the wind blew this afternoon— "Bless the Lord Oh My soul—for all his mercies."

13 Tuesday Yesterday I gave Jane—Mrs. A.— ten dollars—& M. A. Brooks twenty dollars— This is as lovely a day as ever shined—this beautiful day makes me forget the excitement I hear our country is in— I do not see it—only hear a little of it— Great God save our Country from Northern fanatics— Northern sinners— We as a nation have enough to answer for, neither could *we* stand under *Sinai threats*—but *Jesus* pleads for us—& Oh I trust he will prevail—this lovely day from my Heavenly Father to be clouded by man's presumption—No— Jesus can avenge his cause—he can punish as he thinks best—but Oh spare us from those "Northern prey hords." Emma returned the money I lent her to pay Mrs. D. Adams for fowls on Saturday night the 10th Nov. 3.90 cts.

13th To night Dorcas is complaining greatly of sore throat— I am afraid it is scarlet fever sore throat—she complains of its dryness distressing her. I do hope it is only temporary.

Wednesday 14th This is a beautiful day— I am almost tempted to go to Columbia—to see others enjoying themselves—perhaps those who go will not feel happier for having gone.[7] As every thing now stands—I do not feel happy—I don't know though where happiness is to be found— I feel no encouragement to promise myself peace & safety, though my trust is in *God:*— we deserve so little—is the crusher of my hopes.

14th This is a beautiful bright day—the sun shines as lovely as heart could wish it to shine— I wish Lincoln & Hamlin could have died before this & saved our country disolution— The South ought to go out of the U— as it is— Northern Abolitionists hate us so they ought to be glad we are not part of them—*they groaned* to know *we could live*—poor wretches now pray for your own sins & let us answer for ours. Oh that such wretches as No. Abolitionists could be blotted from the records— I hate their principles— I go as much for Patriarchal feelings for *my* or *our* blacks as any one does—but I do

---

7. The State Agricultural Society held its fifth annual fair in Columbia, 13–16 November.

not go for mixing the two races— I ever have lamented their being brought to America— God gave them a country to themselves—& there they ought to have remained— I should not say this, for if God had designed it—he would have had it so—we must believe *his ways are right. Lord help us.*

Thursday 15th A fine day—

16 A good day, only clouds gathering.

Saturday 17 Last night it rained all night—this is a blowing warm day— the clouds look bad—the fair is over & I so mean I could not go to it— I don't know what is to become of poor good for nothing me— I feel as if I was nothing to any *person or thing on earth*—& when any one permits such feelings to master them—they have no interest in any thing on earth. I could not have enjoyed myself in Col——— *at this time*—so why go—'twas sorrow any way. I am too sensitive—yet I would not prefer being otherwise—this feeling makes me hum- ble—what is life after all unless we are made to feel our worthlessness—bouyancy of feeling causes forgetfulness of God. This kind of weather always makes me feel very bad— I am now thinking of Dolly, I hope she may get home safely & better than she has been, in health.[8]

Sunday 18th This is a bright healthy morn—nothing so mean of God's creation as *man*. Mary & Harry asked for papers to go to James H. Adams' this morning— I refused them— I knew 'twas nothing good taking them there. I think it is strange we have such ungovernable spirits— I think I strive to be good, to be a christian, I mean I try to do as I think my Lord & Master would have me to do—but Oh My God this rebel- lious heart— I mourn over its depravity & *wonder* why God does not help me up—when I so ardently desire to do bet- ter—sometimes I feel a ray of comfort—then all is banished & I am disconsolate for my short comings— Why is it so— Oh my God! am I so lukewarm that thou permitest Satan to come between thee & me? Oh My God remember thy ser- vant is only frail human nature—an unworthy vessel—have mercy on me & fashion me to thy will— Oh have mercy & draw me to thee & do not let despair drag me to Hell— Oh

---

8. Dolly was a Sand Hills slave who perhaps had been undergoing treatment at the Fair-Huot clinic in Columbia.

A portrait of Keziah as a young lady, obviously the work of an
itinerant artist who added face and hands to a pre-painted torso.

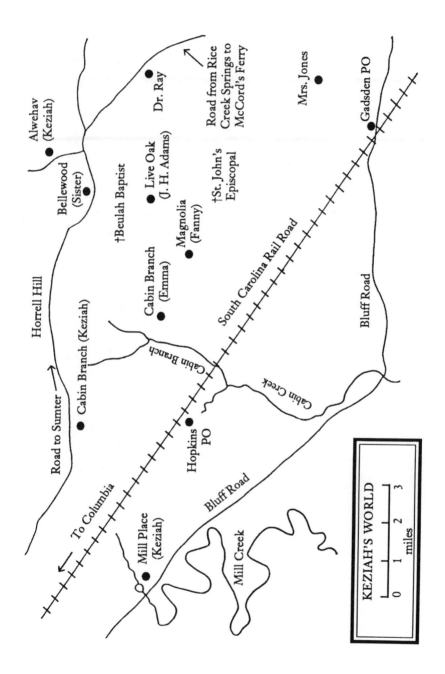

KEZIAH'S WORLD

Road to Sumter

To Columbia

Horrell Hill

Cabin Branch (Keziah)

Alwehav (Keziah)

Bellewood (Sister)

†Beulah Baptist

Cabin Branch (Emma)

Live Oak (J. H. Adams)

Dr. Ray

Magnolia (Fanny)

†St. John's Episcopal

Road from Rice Creek Springs to McCord's Ferry

Mrs. Jones

Gadsden PO

Cabin Branch

Cabin Creek

South Carolina Rail Road

Bluff Road

Hopkins PO

Mill Place (Keziah)

Bluff Road

Mill Creek

0   1   2   3
miles

The northern facade of Keziah's Sand Hills home, now known as Alwehav.

This William Scarborough portrait of William Hopkins now is
owned by great-grandson Theodore J. Hopkins, Jr., of Columbia.

Emma Hopkins, William's wife, Keziah's best friend, cousin, and confidante.

January. Turkeys

February — To save the trouble of looking over the Book — I will here note down the Turkeys I have killed since fall.

Oct 9th one Gobler. Old one.
Mrs Dias Miss Saf — Mrs H & Mrs A & all the children.

22 of Nov — Mrs Williamson E. A. A. & I one Old Gobler

Dec 8 — One of Mrs Purys Goblers. Emma A J —

Dec 18 — Jane & daughter one of last summer Gob= lers.

Dec 22 one of Last years Goblers thinking G — would dine with me — he went to J. H Adams's.

Dec 28 — Janes family a gobler.

Jan 5th Old Gobler — E H J H. Amy H — Fanny A & Joel Adams & Good rays.

Feb 4 one of Mrs Purys Goblers

23 of October one T. Hen

Mrs H & Miss Thickburg spent this day with me 23 of Oct /60.

Oct 20th /60 Cooked a Turkey to day — Sister John came just as my dinner was over & I sent some of this turkey & some jelly to Sister by her servant John. I went to Emmas this afternoon.

Feb 7th This day killed a fine gobler one of Mrs Dickings.

Found a Turkey sitting on 12 eggs on the 4th of Feb S. C — roasted the turkey to day that was killed on the 7th I am all alone I must send part of it to Sister.

After Mrs Jones came on Thursday 14th I had a Gobler killed for din= ner the next day — 15th This one of Miss Mary H turkeys.

28 of march I had one of Mrs Purys finest young yellow gobler for dinner — Mary Brook Jane — Ada, Amy Miss Thern= bert — David Hopkins & three children here.

These "accounting" pages of Keziah's diary deal, not with day-by-day events, but (above) turkeys and (right) eggs collected and distribution of flour and sausages.

I wish to notice thow many eggs
I am to get this year. 1861
January & 0th day — eggs 8
Jan. 3rd ... Do. 7
Sunday 1st in Jan 1861 the
6th day of the month — Phillis
Howards. Old Fanny. Yellow
Fanny. William 9th — out
at the Sands Hills this day.

Sunday 6th eggs	9
Monday 7th Do	5
Tuesday 8 Do	7
Thursday —10 Do	9
Friday 11 Do	7
Saterday 12th 4 eggs	46
Monday 14 6 eggs	121
	167
Tuesday 16 3 eggs	
Wednesday 16th 11 eggs	
Thursday 17 5 eggs	
Friday 18 Eggs	
Sunday 20 13 eggs	
Tuesday 22 17 eggs	
Wednesday 23 9 eggs	
Thursday 24 4 eggs	
Saterday 26 9 eggs	
Monday 28 3 eggs	
Tuesday 29th 30 eggs	167 eggs
Friday 1st of Feb 21 eggs	
Saterday 2nd 12 eggs	
Sunday 3 11 eggs	44

The 1st day of January
/61 I brought down a
cwt lb bag of 1st qual-
ity to 'Ours' — the bag
previous to this did not
last one month. I now
have twelve bags up
stairs — I must be more
economical.

February 1st /61
I have at this time 303 links
of sausages. Three hundred
& three links of sausages.
Feb 22 — I took thirty one of
these links to Emmas for chany
Took out 12 links on Friday
15th of March.
Saterday 23 March I sent two
bags of Shorts to Cabin
branch — these to give
out one is for C Branch
one for the mill. 23 of March

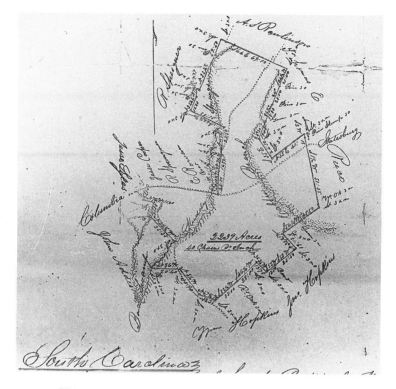

This 1857 survey by Thomas Veal of lands Keziah inherited
from her father is an integral part of her will probated in 1886.

my God help! help! all this day have I been pleading for an interest in thee—still felt dreadful at my distance from thee.

Monday 19th I thank thee Father of mercies for better feelings today—after a night of unpleasant dreams— This is a beautiful day.

20th This is a bright morning— Butter— This morning in the first jar there are eleven balls of butter. These put up for winter—as I take them out I will make how many in this place—

Wednesday 21st This is a sad morning—it has been sleeting a little snow near 10 O'clock— This is a fast day with some— I have no authority from the Bible that any day except Sunday is to be free from work— O how thankful we should be for every moment's blessing.

Thursday 22nd This is a very cold day but not much cloud— Mrs. Williamson from Sumter dined with me this day—her sister Mrs. David Hopkins—Mrs. Gen[l] Hopkins & little Sally all spent this day with me.[9]

Friday 23rd A very cloudy wet day— I came as far as Cabin branch as bad as the weather was—got here in time to see my lard being strained & put into jars— Mrs. R. attended to it until I got here—finished the whole by nine O'clock at night—all pretty white lard except one jar of entrail fat. I have ten jars of lard from this killing of hogs— I did not take the back bone fat.

24 To day had sausages made. I have now 290 links— I think there is another stick not counted in. BEDS. While on this trip I gave Corah (Lydia's daughter), Jenny & Dice—(Hagar's daughter) each home made cloth for bed Cases—it is wide—allow three widths each 2½ yds. long. KGB—

25th Sunday I came to Emma's this morning—a remarkably cold day— Gen[l] Hopkins said the Thermometer was as low as 25 this morning. Mrs. Williamson & Thomas Rembert here to day.[10]

26 Le[f]t Emma's before breakfast—now near 4 O'clock A.M.— still quite cold. I felt thankful & happy after I got home— What a pity that our lives & property are so uncertain to

---

9. Martha Louise Rembert Williamson, sister of Adeline Rembert Hopkins and daughter of Dr. James Rembert. Her diary, also at the South Caroliniana Library, notes she dined with Keziah on 22 November but adds no details.

10. Thomas Rembert, a nineteen-year-old medical student, brother of Mrs. Williamson and Mrs. David Hopkins.

us—it mars my happiness very much when I firmly believe we are in the very midst of enemies— One of my Servants told me (Dick) that Mr. J. E. Reese's dwelling house was burnt before day this morning[11]— I never heard of Mr. R—— suffering from fire before he bought these. . . . . . people—they *were forever burning* the woods while they staid in these Sand Hills—it is a pity he ever bought one of them.

27th Tuesday this day cloudy & wet—had the men burning in the new ground— Harry at C. Branch gathering his corn. Had beets boiled, & made some sause tuesday night.

28 Wednesday Still quite wet & cloudy—all hands in the new ground. I have done very little this day—last night I suffered very much with my arm—tried to spare it to day from too much use of the leaders or mussels. Why is it at times I feel safe as if no dangers were in the distance?— I wish I could feel as free from fear at all times as I do tonight—it is dreadful to dwell on insurrections—many an hour have I laid awake in my life thinking of our danger— Oh God be pleased to prepare me for death & let me die the death of a true christian— seeing & believing as they do. Help us all through this dark vale— O remember my Dear Sister— Oh my God pity such a sufferer—she is in thy hands, O be merciful—*unworthy as we all are*— help us all from these low grounds & give us bright hopes of Heavenly blessings—draw all reluctant hearts—pass not by my dear brother who has so many excellent traits of character, yet has not found an interest in Christ, our blessed intercessor— Oh Lord—remember all my dear relatives & friends & my servants—comfort them— May the latter know that the same God rules all & will be with all who try to obey his commands.

Thursday 29 Last night it was raining whenever I woke—this morning was misty & cloudy— This is a beautiful bright night—the moon is shining. I measured Ned & John's corn this morning, John had one bushel & a half & three parts of a half bushel /// ¾ this no. of half bushels. Ned had seven bushels—//////////// half bushels.[12] I put this in the Old pantry— will notice how long it will last my poultry. I have ten guineas. More than one hundred fowls (dung hill), twenty

---

11. Jesse Reese, age sixty, a well-to-do local planter.
12. These are tally marks, each one representing a half bushel.

four turkeys & seventeen geese. One peck in the day is not sufficient—homney & the lot of rye helps them on. This day I received a letter from my Dear Sister—Peggy Brevard—why is it a letter from her makes me sad?[13] I contrast my feelings with hers & think her so much happier than I am—she has more to interest her with the world than I have—a good daughter—intelligent & well informed—a Son in law whom she may be proud off & bright Grand Children growing up around her—all these make her live her youth over— I do not envy my sister—no—no— but she has been a useful woman while I have been a blank—my nature makes me shrink where I should not— Sister P——— is retiring too—but she has a mind that need not shrink from any other—but mine is far behind hers in every way—even culture could never bring mine paralel— this is another damper to me, I dislike to shew my inferiority in intellect— But I love her dearly & do not envy her— though I would like to be more like her in all her noble qualities. I love Rebecca too & wish I could see more of them.[14] Sister P——— asks me so kindly to go & be with them—I wish I could be there without the trouble to get there—I know I should enjoy their company.

Friday 30th This is a bright cold morning—wind tolerably high. Had coffee parched by Sylvia this morning.

13. Margaret Conner Brevard, widow of J. Franklin Brevard (1788–1829), Keziah's brother-in-law.

14. Rebecca Brevard (1823–1904), daughter of Peggy and J. Franklin Brevard, married Robert I. McDowell. Their son, Franklin McDowell, mayor of Charlotte from 1887 to 1891, handed that office over to a Brevard cousin, a son of Theodore Brevard, who served from 1891 to 1895.

December
"Who can love those whose highest ambition is to cut our throats."

Saturday 1st of December 1860 Where will I be this day one year hence? & Oh what is my Country to pass through between this day & at that time? I know not how to pray—or what to pray for, at times I am so worn with anxiety—sometimes I think all will be peaceful—but when I know the selfishness of the best of men I fear—I dread— Oh God let me *never never* fall into the hands of man—but prepare me for Heaven & help me to be prepared to go when thou callest— Oh God save me from man!!! If our States become divided will not a rebellion soon show distracting heads—yes poor man you know not your own motives until tried—even a committee for this convention has not been nominated quietly— Oh God can we not judge from this what is to be—a worm in the germ— Save us Oh my God—

1st This is a very cold day & clouds looming in the North—but O God thy wrath is mercy in disguise—

> Behind a frowning providence
> God hides a smiling face—

But man's face can never be relied on—all is hidden to suit his own purposes— I am sorry to have such an opinion of human nature— Lord help— Oh help my Country. I feel & know we shall have noble spirits in our cause—so were there in the french revolution—but how feeble they found themselves in the hour of trial.

Sunday 2nd of Dec. This is a briliant day—very cold— I walked out after breakfast—found the ground frozen— I have been reading my Bible & religious papers— I am too cold— Would that I could feel more spiritually minded than I have to day. Near me lies Sister P. letter, if I had suitable paper I would answer it—perhaps conversing with her might kindle better feelings within me— I have no *bad feelings* to day in mind but a lukewarmness— I wish I was all real in my Redeemer's cause—I must wait, hoping the day will brighten as I advance in life.

3 of Dec. How very variable our days are in appearance, yesterday was bright & very cold—this morning the clouds looked like snow—now near midday—still cloudy— Bad news of the Plantation— Titus again in a rogueish shape—united with Mr. Hopkins' negroes & been killing his—Gen[l] Hopkins' hogs—that boy is determined to come to a *bad end*— this is the second daring act in this year— I am sorry to know it— but better know it than have him carrying on as he has— I had had assurances from a good source that he has been taking quantities of whiskey to my plantation—he must get it from some white person. I do feel I ought to sell him. This morning received a letter from H[arriet] Russell.

Tuesday 4th Warmer this morning— I went to Cabin branch & gave cloth to the children & gave Violet a Bed case of home made cloth 7½ yds—this is wide cloth, 3 breadths to a bed—late in the evening I went to Emma's.

5th Wednesday all day at Emma's, she was engaged in having sausages, puddings &c., &c. made.

6 Thursday Morning left Emma's, called at Cabin branch & gave out to the last three on the plantation—now every soul at Cabin branch— have all their cloth for winter— Old & young— Large & Small. I am so glad they all are made comfortable. My negroes say they all *sleep warm*.

Friday 7 Had Cuffe's P. made[1]— I all day trying to fit a sack pattern. This day the weather began to moderate.

Saturday 8th This morning I weighed Ned's fodder 248 lb.—John's 97 lb.—Dick's 132 lb.— A fine morning—sent Harry to Mrs. R——— Adams' twice to day—he got one dozen eggs for me from Mrs. A——— at 15 cts.—he got this afternoon from Mrs. Strictland & Mrs. Adams fourteen doz. for Emma at 25 cts. per doz.[2]— E. is due Mrs. S. & A——— 50 cts.—sent three dollars. Emma—Amy & Sally dined with me to day—had the cold ham baked over, it was fine— Had a young gobler, one of Mrs. Perry's—nice cabbage—turnips—rice, home made Irish potatoes—Sweet Carolinas—back bone & sausages. Who could ask for more,

---

1. Cuffee, an elderly slave aided by Keziah from time to time. This probably means she had a pillow (P.) made for her. Keziah's domestic notes also indicate she was keeping a small sum of money for Cuffee.
2. Mrs. Henry Strickland, a neighbor, and Rebecca Adams, another neighbor mentioned occasionally throughout the diary.

Oh how blest we are—how thankful we should be. Lord I remember thou has promised to be "round about thy people." I trust we are thine, though unworthy servants. I sat up late this night, Night's crown is briliant to night.[3]

9 Sunday Morning Bright & cool— I design going to church this day. I went to church—heard Mr. Beverly—he made a most excellent long prayer & a right good sermon—he alludes too much to the crisis in prospect— I know that God will do the thing he intends—but I hope he will not forget our poor natures, we are in his hands— Oh God spare us awhile, though as a nation we do deserve chastisement— Lord remember us in mercy!! Met Mrs. Jones at church—she feels & believes as I do—

Monday 10th This is a blustering day— I am really uneasy about fire— I must send & hear from Sister—poor Sister, but perhaps you are as happy as I am—all comforts are from God & he blesses his own as they deserve. I hope & trust in God as soon as Secession is carried out—we of the South begin to find a way to get all the Negroes sent back to Africa & let the generations to come after us live in more peace than we do— I can't see how we are ever to be safe with them in our midst— I wish every soul of them were in Africa contented in their own homes—let us begin on corn bread & live in peace & security—as long as they are here & number so many more than the whites there is no safety any way— Men of the South—I fear our end is near & the Yankeys will glory over their work. I do hate a Northern Abolitionist— Lord forgive me—but who can love those whose highest ambition is to cut our throats.

11th Tuesday This is a cold blowing disagreeable day— I came to Cabin branch to attend to lard, filled eight jars with lard this time. Ten the first killing, 18 jars.

12 Wednesday very cold but not so bad a day as yesterday was. Making sausages to day—put some Old lard in one of my new jars to day.

13th A beautiful—& pleasant day. I am still at Cabin branch— I believe I had as well stay here as any other place—while here I know I am free from intruders— I can be as much to my-

---

3. The Corona Borealis, an elliptical ring of stars, also known as the Northern Crown.

self as I wish— I like the company of friends & those I love— I care very little for any other company.

14 A Cloudy ugly day & quite cold— Mr. R has taken 28 bags of cotton to Col. to day. I hope he may get enough to pay my taxes & D^{rs}' bills & over— Many a D^r bill is paid for very little pain— I know by my arm— I might have run this arm up to 100 dollars if I had consulted feelings— I thought I would try time & care, nature's remedies— I hope it will cure in truth—it certainly is better— I have drank Saras-parelli & used Dr Tally's liquid for rubbing.

15 Saturday It commenced sleeting before day—there was no great
Morning deal of sleet, it ceased early in the morning— I left the plantation after 12 O'clock & got safe to the Sand Hill— 'twas remarkably cold & found more ice here than I left at Cabin branch. The No. side of every house sleeted with ice—locks & doors of two houses fronting the No. so cased with ice they were hard to open— I had to have hot water for one lock.

16 Sunday The ice has thawed some, the No. side of the tops of four houses still white, now 3 O'clock A.M.—where the sun could shine on any thing it has disappeared—still very cold & to-night I can see to the E. & S. & I do not see a cloud of any kind—this morning while out—the skies were batted over pretty much with white clouds.[4] Lord how long are we to be so blest, as to sit around our own comfortable firesides? Oh God make us worthy to deserve them & Oh change the hearts of all sinners that we may enjoy these blessings to thy glory— This morning nature was beautifully tinselled & we were permitted to look on it from comfortable chambers— Oh God spare us this previlege & make us all thine is my *prayer.*

Monday 17th This day had the two upper fowl houses scalded & cleaned—this day quite cold again—ice melted from the North side of the house—received a note from Jane Adams to day saying she would spend tomorrow with me. 17th— $13.35 cts. in my purse after paying D[ick], N[ed] & John. Paid this (87½ cts.) for lard (Ned) leaf lard.[5] This is right, 7 lb. of l[eaf] lard at 12½ cts. per lb.

---

4. The sky looked like cotton batting, filling used in quilts.
5. Lard made from leaf fat, the highest quality of fat, which was found near the kidneys of hogs.

Tuesday 18 This day tolerably bright—still quite cold. Mrs. Jas. H. Adams—Janie—Laura—Ellen, Caroline & Jimmy spent to day with me. For dinner one of last summer's Goblers, an O[ld] Ham, spare rib pie, brains, back bones & vegetables turnips—Cabbage—rice—Irish potatoes—this is all— Jane is more uneasy about small pox than the affairs of our Country[6]—not so with *me*— I pray to fall into God's hands not man's—man let loose from all restraints is a very *Devil*. I see no hope for us. Oh my God fit me for Heaven & leave me not to hear the dying groans of my Country—it seems to me this was to be & what God orders who can thwart it.

Wednesday 19th This was a drizly morn—all my men servants in the new ground. I see nothing but sad news in the papers. Lord have mercy on the dear south— O that I should have lived to see this sad state of things— God thou canst save us but no other power can do it. 19—I have written two letters to day—one to Sister Peggy, one to Caroline E. Brevard.[7] This whole day has been shrouded in a dense fog—& rain alternately. My shoulder is worse than it has been— I sometimes think I will go out after nine o'clock & see what my servants are doing—it is now after dark— I enquired for Harry & Dick, neither of them are in their houses, I can't think where they are on this wet night. Ned went home this

---

6. This disease had been present in Columbia for nearly a month. On 17 December the *Tri-Weekly Southern Guardian* reported four more cases of smallpox and another four of varioloid (a milder form). During these weeks, Newberry, Yorkville, and Charlotte passed ordinances designed to restrict contact with Columbia. Those informing Newberry authorities of violators received half of any fine collected. Free blacks and slaves who defied the ban might receive a hundred lashes, and the owner of a slave found guilty could also be fined.

7. Caroline Mays Brevard (1811–1892), an Edgefield District native, became the second wife of Theodore W. Brevard in 1831. Theodore (also known as Theodorus and Theodosius), three years younger than Joseph and a graduate of South Carolina College, remained in Columbia to study law. Early in 1826 he married Caroline Hopkins, Keziah's younger sister. In 1830, two years after Caroline's death, this young man qualified to practice in South Carolina and subsequently became a Richland District justice of the peace and law partner of James H. Hammond. However, by 1833 Theodore had moved to Alabama, and the following year he sold his interests in the Lincoln County iron business to Joseph. Theodore later settled in Florida, where he served as state comptroller, 1855–1860. Brevard County is named in his honor.

evening, took my two letters with him. I have just finished a letter to Cousin Mary E. Boykin.

20 Thursday This is a shining day—the wind is high. I have sent Jim—Harry & Ned to work on the road[8]—kept Dick—Joe & John at home—it seems to me I do not realize our danger—although I see nothing to encourage us to hope on.

Friday 21st This morning my nephew J. G. Ross reached my Sand Hill home—a student of Chapel Hill N. Ca—his residence is Desoto [Parish], Louisianna—he is looking pale & thin—fatigued from his last night's travel on the cars. English Hopkins came with him—English returned[9]— I had a hurried dinner, after dinner we walked out to see the garden & poultry. This has been a pleasant day, but Oh how unhappy I feel about my country & my country's rash move—my God—let us get rid of slavery—this is my prayer—never more will there be any security in this land— Lord save us is my constant prayer to Almighty God.

22 Saturday To day I made potatoe custards—sent to Kitterson's & got one dollars worth of Spanish potatoes—paid cash for them— I this day sent to Mrs. Strickland for eggs, got eleven, paid 25 cts.—for them— I also paid Mrs. Strickland fifty cts. that was due by Emma for two doz. eggs, Harry did not pay on Saturday the 8th of this month— Goodwyn dined at James H. Adams' to day—he says the ladies were at home—J. H. A. in Charleston.[10] This is a tolerably pleasant day— Let me not forget to thank my God for all his mercies. Oh God save our Country. I got one doz. eggs from Mrs. D. Adams today & one doz. on the 8th of Dec. not paid for— Mrs. A——— said she would let me have them at 15 cts.— I will not ask it of her—will pay market price. Received a note from Mr Clark to day—he is anxious to rent my house in Col. to Gov. Pickens.[11] I rather think I will oblige him &

8. By law, male residents were supposed to work on the public roads for so many days each year. Until 1865 blacks did most of the labor, whites being able to avoid this onerous duty by subterfuge or payment of a commutation tax in lieu of work.

9. English was attending the University of Virginia at this time.

10. Adams was attending the secession convention, which had moved from Columbia to that city because of the smallpox scare.

11. Edgefield's Francis Pickens (1805–1869) had just been elected governor on the seventh ballot, a victory that ended a sixteen-year "arrangement" alternating the office between upcountry and low. It is not known

rent a small one for myself. I promised to loan Mrs. Strickland some Coffee on Monday. How much I feel for poor people who have large families to struggle for. We who are able ought to help them. Lord give us "goodliness with contentment." Can we doubt God's protection—there have been several houses this week without a white gentleman at home & yet we are safe—has not our God been with us?

23rd This is a raw cloudy day— Goodwyn has gone to St. John's church to be with his cousins—he is a babtised member of the Babtist church— I hope nothing may draw him from his choice church. I am a liberal christian at heart—but the breaking down of Old Beaulah leaves a worm at the core of my good feelings. I try to root it out—why should I care one farthing who goes to St. John's— I don't look to man for comfort— God is my refuge & let me shew by all my course through life—that he is my rock to shelter under in this land. Tomorrow I must perform my promise to one of my poor neighbours:—send her four lb. of coffee. (I never received one ct. for this /61 Dec.)

24th This is a lovely day in appearance—rather cold— Harry paid me for the flour he got & I paid him for the two baskets I got from him—now have eight dollars in paper, 2.30 cts. in silver. I sent Mrs. Strickland four lb. of Coffee—she will pay me in eggs for these—ten lb. of flour I will give to Mrs. S———. Mary A. Kitterson called to day & brought me a nice piece of venison, for which I was really obliged to her. My neighbours though not rich in worldliness are kind & often send me acceptable presents. There is to be a wedding to night near this [place]— Henry Strickland to Mary Adison[12]— I hope they will be quiet & have no noise about it—all things should be done decently *at all times* but particularly so at this time when every heart is throbbing for their country—though I hope & pray for peace, I see nothing to hope for. God almighty let the other states be united

---

if he actually rented Keziah's house. Mr. Clark probably was L. C. Clarke, a prominent bookkeeper, who lived on the north side of Blanding, across the street from Keziah's city residence.

12. Henry Strickland, twenty-three-year-old son of a local farmer bearing the same name, and Mary Addison, age twenty-two, daughter of William Addison. They were the first couple to be married at St. John's Congaree. Mrs. Strickland undoubtedly was borrowing foodstuffs in preparation for this event.

if we can do no good as we are, but I pray the South will not let us be imposed on. Lord! Lord! save us from the assassin—from Northern fanatics. Goodwyn proposes to go to St. John's church tomorrow—I don't feel much like going—though I may do so.

25 This Christmas day— I thank the Heavenly Father for the blessing conferred on us through the scenes of this day 1860 years ago— May we never abuse the blessing—help me O God to do thy will. This has been a cloudy cold day—rain too. Goodwyn did not go to St. John's to day—of course the day was too bad. Jim drove the horses to Cabin branch and brought out the cake—oysters—Oranges—butter &c., &c.— My Country can I forget thee—no—no—Lord save us from sorrows.

26th Wednesday A cold clear day— Goodwyn & myself went to Emma's, dined with her & remained all night.

27 This is a bright cold day— English & Goodwyn—took early breakfast & left for a duck hunt in the swamp—after usual breakfast I came home—this evening since dark Goodwyn got back— I had no thought he would get back this far to-night. I expect company tomorrow— Mary is not well but I must try & do without her— I have custards & jelly ready & I now must make fruit to do for the balance of the disert. Let me never forget God's goodness: is my prayer.

26 The day before yesterday I got a new mouse trap—it has already caught six mice—four last night & two tonight. These six caught in my closet. [In succeeding weeks Keziah kept a running score—in all thirteen mice had been killed by mid-January.]

28 Friday Mrs. James H. Adams with Janie, Laura, Carry, Ellen & Jim spent the day with Goodwyn & myself— Randy's little Jane with them. They brought this morning's paper with them, the "Guardian," from it we read that Ft. Moultrie had been evacuated on the 27th & the Ft. was on fire at 5 O'clock thursday evening.[13] God alone knows the design of it—we are all in the dark as to the future— Oh that this strife could be ended for the good of the whole country— I know not what to think, certainly awful troubles seem hanging over us— My God take me to thee—thou has made me & taken

---

13. Columbia's *Southern Guardian*—daily, tri-weekly, and weekly editions—was published by Charles P. Pelham at 177 Richardson Street.

care of me thus far— Oh take me to thee—rem[em]bering my frailties— I have no right to doubt thy promises. I hoped to see Emma's family to day— I can't imagine what kept them— I expect the news from Charleston makes E———very unhappy. Goodwyn went home with Jane & her daughters this afternoon. I am not so much troubled as I have been— Oh my God I might have been far from these scenes if I had let conscience be my guide— God forgive me for my past sins & let me bow to thee with humility, if my lot is hard hereafter I cannot complain— I have no right to murmur. Had a green ham & a gobler for dinner, piece of corn beef—sausages—irish potatoes—sweet potatoes, rice, greens, turnips—Peach roll—Potatoe custards—jelly—nuts, prunes, oranges, second course. This is a cloudy cold day.

Saturday 29 of This morning very cold & cloudy—a few drops of sleet
Dec./60 before 10 A.M.; now it is 5 mi[nutes] of 11 A.M. & the sun has shewn a dim light, gone again. Oh God save our dear City Charleston—let not a head be bruised by the Northern people—thou canst save us, Oh save us!!! This Old year truely goes out full of trouble. Let better signs soon gleam on us & Oh that 61 could bring peace & love to thy people.

29 It is now bed time & raining briskly— I gave out COFFEE & Bread to be made for my evening meal—when I made a cup & tasted it, it was such stuff I sent word to Rosanna she certainly had spilt the coffee before it got to the pot—what she had sent me was not coffee—'twas such dreadful tasted stuff I sent the cup of coffee to R——— to taste of—she came to me & said something was the matter with it, she did not know what. R——— went again to the kitchen & returned saying some one had ground *salt in the mill*—they threw the coffee away, not one of them could drink it—some of them said it tasted like Alum—some of them said it tasted like terrible stuff— I felt sick a few seconds since—it seems to be all over now—this is the second time—can it be possible it was an attempt to poison—somehow I can't think so. So friends if I should be suddenly taken off after a meal—remember the coffee— I would not have any one injured innocently on mere suspicion— I rather suppose some of my lazy negroes ground salt in it for bread. Now Lord let my last & constant prayer be for my Country— Oh save

Charleston & all her dear people. What a night this would be for all in trouble.

30th of December soon will 1860 be past—forever gone— What has been done in this year for man's blessings! Whoever has not been working for good to others as well as themselves had as well not worked at al[l]— I am sure I do not feel the extent of my own unworthiness. This is a sad morn—cold, wet & dark, nothing to cheer us but the fact we have warm rooms— Yes we have a great deal to make us forget this dismal day without— God still protects us from our cut throat Abolitionists— I will not call them neighbours—they are the selfish & envious sons of *Satan*—not a grain of Christ's charity in their whole body— Oh God do with them as thou thinkest they deserve. God is good & knows all *our hearts*, Oh how thankful I am to have an Omniscent Father. Is our convention safe? is Charleston still protected from our enemies? I hope so & pray God will never suffer things otherwise. Sometimes I am ready & do often say I wish the Africans had never touched our soil—this is a hard wish—those who have come & have had kind masters have been blest—had they been left to this day on Afric's sands their would have been one trouble after another for them—it is only in favoured spots *now* that they are safe from war & slavery in their own country.

30th My Dear Sister are you lonely this disagreeable day? I hope not— God can bless you as he blesses me, I am content here alone— I feel it is such a privilege to be quiet & have good company in good books that I seldom feel ennui. Bible. The Hebrew ceased to be the living language of the Jews during the Babylonish captivity—all Jewish productions after that period were written either in the Chaldee or Greek. It is now dark & I have finished my evening repast— I have not witnessed such a day of rain in a long while—the rain has fallen with very few & short intervals throughout the day & frequently 'twas a fast rain— I think the members of the Convention have had a discouraging time—but I pray the sun may beam on them more cheeringly after this—the certainty of a peaceful adjustment of things would be glorious news. Goodwyn has returned from Jane's as bad as the evening is. Rain still pouring at 8 O'clock at night.

31st Last night a dismal night—it rained incessantly & the wind was high— I was awake several times—my arm was very painful— This is a *sad, sad* looking day— Oh that the genial sun could pierce the dark, foreboding clouds. I woke dreaming an alarming dream—thought singular clouds were flitting over my head while I stood near the old brick oven of my mother's—while these clouds were fearful over head—I saw in the S.E. corner of the yard two raging, smoking fires, the flames bursting high at intervals— I thought I called aloud & ordered the fires to be put out, the fright woke me— Lord save me from trouble. Save me from anger & all that is amiss in thy sight. This is the last day of 1860—am I nearer my God than I was one year ago? I am nearer my end & I trust my faith in Jesus is a more conforting faith as I grow older— I now know Jesus to be altogether lovely & trust by striving to do his will he will remember me in mercy. Oh My God save this dear Country & make us all thy truthful servants— this is my prayer— Lord hear me— Lord remember my relatives this day wheresoever they may be—bless my sister & brother especially & comfort my afflicted nephew—but above all spare our Country. Now about 2 O'clock A.M.—& all gloom without— My Country!!! My Country!!!

January
"I see nothing ahead but trouble."

This is the first day of 1861 I opened my Bible at the CXVII & CXVIII Psalm—have read the two—great encouragement in these Psalms— "The Lord is on my side; I will not fear: What can man do unto me." I trust the Lord is on our side in this national strife— Oh that he would say to the North *be just* & to the South *be just*—they both err in God's sight— Man is very imperfect. The 1st day of January was a cloudy, disagreeable day—no rain unless a drizzle in the morning—Emma sent for Goodwyn & myself to go over—we went late, got to E. just before dark— Ned drove us with the mules in the Old Carriage—it commenced raining again after night.

Wednesday 2nd It rained dreadfully to day some intervals— I don't know when I have seen so much rain as has fallen in a few days— remained at Emma's all day.

3rd Thursday We left Emma's this morning—came by the plantation— straightened all my accounts & papers with Mr. Rawlinson—called to see old Lettuice—left her some coffee, sugar & one plug of tobacco. Got home to the Sand Hills about 1 O'clock, had dinner— After 10 O'clock it brightened up & I had high hopes of good weather—this afternoon is again cloudy— Oh my Dear Dear Country are you to be torn asunder to gratify Northern prey birds. *God—Almigh—ty* save us!!! To day Frank offered to pay for what he owed me—said the cows (not my cows) had destroyed his crop— I forgave him the debt. 3rd of January—Thursday—now bed time, all the stars are out & I do hope the bad weather is over. Jesus Master—save us from *our enemies.*

4th Friday This is the first bright day since the 26 of Dec. that was a clear day—since then nature seems to have wept over our fate— We are hoping to visit to day—call & see Sister, perhaps go farther. Dorcas has commenced a quilt. I've gave [sic] her the scraps. Lord—Lord place my thoughts on eternity & keep them fixed on that theme—then Lord Jesus we may hope to meet the crisis as thy children—with help from thee we can get through this trouble—if thou withhold thy aid we are undone—undone.

5th Saturday Still good weather—rather cold—yesterday afternoon Goodwyn & myself spent with Sister—before sundown we left Sister & went to James H. Adams' to spend the night— Met Mr. & Mrs. Hinkle—Mrs. Mcelhany, these nice persons all of them[1]— Came home early this morning. I was expecting company to dine—James Hopkins—English Hopkins—Amy & Sally Hopkins—Joel Adams & his sister Fany spent the day with Goodwyn & myself.[2] I had an old Ham boiled ('twas brought out before Christmast) & a fine old Gobler, he was killed on New Year's day—the best tasted turkey I have had. All the stars bright this night. January 5th It seems to me we surely are not to be involved in a bloody war. Lord place my affections on Heavenly things. I pray that God will comfort our men & watch over them through their troubles. Oh make them watchful over themselves & over their country's cause, "Unless the Lord keep the City, the watchman will sleep."

January 6th "Thy mercy O Lord endureth forever: Forsake not the works of *thine own hands*." Sunday morning—this is a moderately cool day—sun shines dimly—still pleasant enough— Communion day at our church this day— I wish I was present to hear Dr Thornwell[3]— I do love his sentiments on such occasions—he is encouraging, at the same time makes no allowance for *sins*—which if God is just—& he is, all must be so— Yes I love to sit & listen to God's words at all times from any one whom I believe to be a truely pious man— I prefer being in my own church first—then the Babtist— Goodwyn has gone to hear Mr. Hankle at St. John's church—Mrs. Ray's & Jane['s] church— Their family can't go back far in their church— This is none of my business &

---

1. William H. Hanckel was rector of St. John's Congaree. Mrs. Mcelhany cannot be identified.

2. This group of young people probably includes James Hopkins (1839–1904), a medical student in Charleston and the older brother of English, Amy, and Sally (not James Tucker Hopkins, Fanny's son), Robert Joel Adams (1843–1862), and his sister, Frances (1846–1895).

3. James H. Thornwell (1812–1862), who vacillated between academic and religious realms throughout much of his life, was president of South Carolina College from 1851 to 1855, when he accepted a professorship at Columbia's Presbyterian Theological Seminary. A political moderate and conservative until 1860, he then became an ardent Confederate.

it is a trifling thing for me to think of this on this day. God forgive me— for caring one ct. who left Beaulah— God can once more cause her to spread forth her branches if she deserves to flourish—if she is sunk in sin, her case is hopeless— O my God change my heart & make me worship thee in truth—this is my heart's desire— When I awake in the night my first thought is, "My state is out of the Union"— when I think of it, I feel we really cannot work— I wish this thing was ended & let us know our lot— Lord God— Almighty!!! forsake not the works of thine *own hands:*—we are thine—bless the Lord, *we are thine.* O God say to the North thus far and no far-ther— We of the South have no desire to interfere with others—we try to wash out our own sins—& leave each one to answer to God for *their own sins.*

Monday 7th This is not a bright day—a little warmer & a dull sunshine—last evening Goodwyn brought a letter to me—letter from Harriet R. Russell—Marietta, Georgia. 'Tis now after 1 O'clock P.M. Goodwyn has just left me—he will take the Car at Hopkins T[urn] Out at 4 O'clock—will I ever see my nephew again? God alone knows— If I should never meet him in this world, O God permit us all to meet hereafter in a world *free from sorrow*—a world where selfish man has no part nor lot— O my God take care of him & return him a good vessel to his dear family—father—mother—sisters & brothers & all the other dear & near relatives. My God I will not cease to plead for my country!!! The sun grows dim—I fear we shall have rain before morning. I gave my nephew before we parted fifty dollars which shall never come against him if I should have anything to leave when I die—all belongs to God—my stewardship lasts so long as he pleases & no longer— Lord help me to act so as to render in a good account when I am called on by thee. I was rejoiced to hear J. H. A———— my nephew was improving in health— My Master let him not forget his first duty to *thee:*— "Lord forsake not the works of *thine own hands*" Psalms.

8 of January Amy Adams called to see me this morning—rather after 12
Tuesday O'clock asking aid to buy arms for the fork company[4]— I promised $20. In my heart I was opposed to breaking up

---

4. The term "the fork" has several meanings on the local scene, but in this instance it undoubtedly refers to the area south of the road to Sumter and east of Tom's Creek.

this beautiful union of ours—but I must act for my home, the home of my forefathers for three generations—they came from England & fought against her in our struggle for right & justice. This is a fine bright pleasant day. Goodwyn is now, I hope, safe at the University of No. Ca., Chappel Hill. Lord watch over him. Lord watch over our once favoured country—but above all give us clean hearts. This morning I received a letter from Epps Wharton of Louisiana.[5] I do wish it had come yesterday so Goodwyn could have heard from home. Amy Adams thinks our slaves will be faithful to us in the crisis should it come— I think we all have some, the fewest in No., who would not butcher us—but I am sure most of them would aim at freedom—'tis natural they should & they will try for it. O that God would take them out of bondage in a peaceable way—let no blood flow—we are attached to our slaves—they are as our own family & would to day have been a happy people if Northern fanaticism had not warred against us. I have walked through the clearing twice to day. I am not happy & cannot think myself safe—every time I wake in the night I think of my State being out of the Union—if my voice could have prevented [it]—it would never have ceceded alone—as to Florida what is she—a poor State at best & settled mostly by Carolinians— I think G[oodwyn] is now in his room reading—he commenced the life of Jackson while visiting with me.

Wednesday I left home early, went to Sister's—left Sister's about eleven
morning the O'clock & went to Cabin branch—took dinner & went in the
9th afternoon to Emma Hopkins'—spent the night at Emma's— This was a bright day—moderate in temperature, but the wind blew quite strong after 10 O'clock A.M.

Thursday 10 Left Emma's this morning after breakfast— A remarkably high wind all this day—though it did not blow as strong after 2 O'clock P.M.—it blew on till near sun down— Last night we received the news of the Star of the West—from Charleston[6]— O God put it into the hearts of the Northern

---

5. Keziah Epps Goodwyn Wharton (born 1826), daughter of Keziah's half-brother Jesse and thus an aunt of Goodwyn Ross.

6. The *Star of the West* was an unarmed merchant ship secretly dispatched by President Buchanan to reinforce Union forces in Charleston Harbor. When fired upon, the vessel withdrew. It subsequently was captured by the Confederates in April of 1861.

people to do right & let us once more shew to the world we can yield to all that is right in thy sight— We have never invaded Northern rights—all we want is *right* in its plainest sense. Mr. R. told me to day he still had sixty dollars of my money in his hands. I hope to lay vanity aside this year & make good use of my money:—that is, do real good with it. I have sent on two hundred & fifty dollars to my relative James E. Goodwyn in Mowcow, Arkansas, as a present[7]— he is very needy & I pray this may put him above want & put him in a way to live comfortably. It is my desire to try to be more economical through this year sixty-one— Lord help me to do all that may be acceptable in thy sight. KGHB.

Friday 11 Sun shines dimly, very cold. Ned & John commence throwing down corn beds—where I am to sow oats. Horses gone to be shod. Harry in the new ground with Sam & Tom. Dorcas inclined to talk more than work— Mary & Sylvia sewing—the two latter do about the one fourth of what one person should do—those who have negroes to manage are Jobs or should be—they have almost as great trials as he had. I rather think the clouds will soon predominate over the sunshine. No wind this morning. Citizens of Charleston has God saved our City through the night? He will do as he pleases & if he condescends to save you—what returns will you strive to make him— Lord the blessing can not be returned by man—the glory is thine— Blessed be the *Lord— God—Almighty!!!* Now half after three O'clock P.M., quite cloudy—we have had only occasional sun light through this day, still quite cold. I feel that I neglect reading too much— I hope we may have better times—when that is ascertained I will try to do more good & live more like a rational being than I have heretofore done—if I had been torpid all my life I would have been as useful— God gave me powers & means & I have acted the coward more than the willingly useful servant.

12 Saturday Another dim day—occasional gleams of sunshine—not very cold—if every month through this year corresponds with

---

7. James Epps Goodwyn (born 1841), eldest son of Francis Epps Goodwyn III and grandson of Keziah's uncle, Francis Epps Goodwyn (born c. 1766). Keziah apparently means Moscow, a small community in Jefferson County near Pine Bluff.

these 12 days, we are to have a year of gloom—when the sun is shrouded in clouds our hearts are sad— I have not been happy to day—still every thing goes wrong—the uncertain state of our Country is dreadful— O my God end this dreadful suspense. My arm very painful last night— Now near 8 O'clock at night— *God* save our dear country & make us all followers of thy dear son—then we shall be happy— we want no Northern fanaticism—we want—*the love of Christ in our souls* [so] that we love the brethren & do unto others as we would have others do to us—.

13 Sunday This is a cold cloudy morn— I am sorry to know how seldom I go to Church— If I live I hope in time their will be a church nearer to me. Lord send others to encourage Mr. Beverly—but thy works are not dependent on man— O God help up our only hope here— Beaulah pour out thy spirit & let its *stones* speak— I wish not to pull down others but Oh help up the church of our forefathers—let us never be ashamed of what they reared & consecrated to thy service. We have more scripture for its ordinances than those of any church *under the Heavens* & now Lord let it flourish like a vine planted near the river of water.—he who will search the scriptures with his *soul set* on *truth*—must acknowledge if one church is nearer right than another it must be the babtist—but we believe not in a saving privilege in one more than another— Christ said the time would come when ye shall neither "in the mountain, nor yet at Jerusalem, worship the Father." "But the hour cometh, & now is, when the true worshipers shall worship the Father in spirit & in truth; for the Father seeketh such to worship him."

14th Mr. Rawlinson came out this morning— I was alarmed to see him, in these stirring times any thing out of the ordinary routine of things alarms— Oh God I thank thee & I know all hearts thank thee for saving us to this hour—we are in thy hands—continue Heavenly Father to keep us in the *hollow of thy Hands*. All nature is cased in ice this morning & all looks pretty— I would *add grand*—if the sun could break through the dense clouds & shine in splendour while the trees are garbed in ice 'twould be a briliant display of God's works— Oh that it would— I would put on warm shoes & walk out to enjoy the sight. I wish to keep in mind that I have promised to try to be economical this year—not to indulge in luxuries & make the clothing I have do me—add nothing to my household furniture until our country settles down in peace & happiness— I pray I may be firm enough to keep this *promise*. Lord help me to do whatsoever is right in thy sight. 14th of Jan./61 K. B————d. My journal is poor— I am obliged to note down many things or my memory would lead me into errors, for that reason I keep this little memorandum book—sometimes it relieves dull moments to note down items. This day received a letter from Caroline Brevard in Pensacola—she asks me to unite with her in prayer for *her sons* & our Country—with all my heart O my God do I pray for this dear Country & C———— I pray your sons may be watched over through this struggle—& every son who has to risk his life in the cause. All is gloom to me— We have had a dense fog for nearly this whole day—the ice has melted from the trees near the house. The negroes say it has not melted in the woods.

Tuesday 15th   No vestige of the sleet to be seen this morning—still a thick fog until 12 O'[clock] Mid-day— Now the trees are quite visible—yet very doubtful whether 'twill rain or shine. Let us pray that our countrymen far & near may put down *self* & do for their country's good— I fear man is too selfish to be just & charitable—can I hope to see our country in peace again? Oh God save us—put it into the hearts of our people to do right— Let those who are to guide our little bark remember those on whom the burden falls—the soldiers who are to do the hard work for So. Ca.———— Lord remember them—& let their trials soon be ended that they may soon return to peace & usefullness. I have been looking out at the window—the smoke in the clearing is going up as strait as a pine, this must be a sign the rain is over although there are clouds East. Now dark, I saw the new moon while walking in the clearing since the sun went down. My Country! My Country!! Can it be—are you to be the prey of designing men—

Wednesday 16th   Last night was an alarming time— The wind blew terrible blasts— I had my men waked & sent them to the clearing to put out the fires, I was alarmed but I knew I was blessed compared to the soldiers & Citizens of Charleston— Oh that God would put into the hearts of his children to try to make peace with each other—we who are remote from towns are saved a great deal in feelings—danger may be as near but we do not know it & when it comes, if it should, we will be spared a thousand pangs those who are in cities have to feel—'twill be sooner over with us—but God is our ruler—in him we hope:—if we deserve his protection—he will save us. Northern Abolitionists, I tell you if we could get rid of slavery on humane terms, we could shew you our hearts are good, yea a thousand times better than yours— I have no doubt we have some brute masters—but you know not what we have to bear from a bad negro— I have slaves under my care—some are very good, never give the least trouble—but I have a few terrible spirits to keep in order—some we manage by kindness, some nothing but the fear of punishment will restrain in the least. The wind is still high now at 10 O'clock P.M.—but we are blessed with a bright & glorious sunshine—what we have seen & felt very little off since the 1st day of January. It has continued blowing through this day— I really wished to go to J. H. A——— to day—the high wind kept me at home. Mary & myself made potatoe custard to day—succeeded very well with the pastry. Ned thinks they have thrown down the corn beds—half through the ground I intended for oats. Joe—Harry & Jim raked up leaves in the clearing to day. I really must stop Charley & Roach from going into the rye.[8]

17 Thursday Sun shines dimly this morning. Mrs. Kitterson sent her little daughter—I really do not know whether it is Lizy or Margaret—I seldom see them & cannot recollect them, the two near one height & I not intimate with them, sometimes call them right, sometimes wrong—the servants say this one was Miss Lizy, to borrow five dollars—this is the second five dollar bill I have loaned Mrs. Kitterson.[9] All my hands at the fence around the rye this morning—Last night I suffered very much with my arm & back—have a slight head ache this morning— I am all ignorance in our public concerns for several days— I pray God is working out our safety— Lord Jesus intrude for us. At night. This day quite unexpectedly Cousin Ady [Ada], Amy & Sally came between twelve & one o'clock—I was sitting at table partaking of a very homely dinner— I made them sit around & join me taking it as lunch for them— I had another dinner got—'twas late before we partook of it as it was commenced so late, however I had

---

8. Charlie and Roach were the names of horses owned by Keziah.

9. At this time, Elizabeth was twelve, Margaret fourteen.

half a ham boiled, a chicken pie made & sausages fried, rice, sweet potatoes & loaf bread—potatoe pudding, fruit & nuts— How blest we are! in a few days, perhaps hours, what a change may come over us. We may be reduced to begery—but Oh My God save us—spare us Lord—& see if we cannot, will not serve thee better— O God save us from sheding the blood of our fellow man— O God save us for Jesus sake, I know he pleads for us. This day throughout has been cloudy. My Country!! Oh My Country!!

Friday 18th Now half after 10 O'clock A.M., it commenced raining by day light & is still raining, a great deal of rain has fallen this morning— Our poor soldiers, I trust in God you are protected from the inclemency of the weather— Oh my God bring about a reconciliation between the N. & the S———— or let the war begin & end as soon as possible— Oh God do not let the N———— trample us under their will— sooner let every white face in the S———— die on his soil than be subject to those who hate us for they know not what— Lord, Lord how long have many of us clung to the North—hoping there was not so much cause to complain— but Lord—Lord what have we come to by being oppressed—now plunged into a war— Oh God Almighty save us—save us— I do not depend on man— *My God is my all.* Still pouring down rain. I am due Harriet a letter & Caroline Brevard of Pensacola— I wish I had a heart to do any thing— My Dear Dear Sister, I heard from her this afternoon—she is still trying to hire her poor negroes[10]—poor poor Sister, Oh the sorrows you have passed through!!— why is it that some of God's children are so crushed on this earth?—perhaps the trials of one are for the good of many— if we neither see, nor feel these troubles we forget God, & Satan leads us to our ruin. My God our troubles while on earth are severe—still they might be worse & amid all our trials we have a great deal to be thankful for— Lord Jesus intrude for our dear country & thy rebellious children. My arm pains me—the right side of my throat seems to have the same feelings at times & then down near my back bone—my right side is more pained than the other— I think it is my throat. Friday night.

---

10. According to the 1860 census, Sarah owned twenty-one slaves.

19th Saturday The sun is shining although the weather is not settled—&
'tis much colder this morning than it has been for several
days—my arm not as painful last night, I mopped my throat
yesterday evening. Lord I thank thee for saving us through
the night— Lord continue to watch over us & help *me* to
stronger faith in this hour to try us. I hope to get to see
James H. Adams this morning— I have been anxious to visit
him all the week—friday it rained—Thursday I had company, Wednesday & Thursday the wind was too high for me
to venture out with my horses— I am a little afraid of them.
This day have Harry, Ned—Sam & Tom cutting the large
oak in the Cow pen.

20th Yesterday afternoon I went to see James H. Adams, he was
at home—his family had gone visiting— I *went* on to Mrs.
F. M. Hopkins' & sat with her till near sun down— I found
Mrs. Ray & three little girls with her— Fanny as usual much
engaged with her front lawn & garden— I think enlarging
the yard has improved it very much— I have often thought
a large house should have a large lawn in front & at the
ends— I spent the night at James H. Adams'—poor man, I
do feel for him & cannot see how any one can say he looks
well—his eyes are changed & shew plainly he is a sufferer—
Oh I hope he may be spared for a long time— I am so thankful he has become pious & pray Heavenly Father thou wilt
perfect the good work began in him— I think he has a poor
opinion of Frank Pickens' management of public affairs[11]—
Oh Father of mercies help us all & let some thing be done to
check mobocracy. Lord save us from being overpowered by
our enemies at the North. Nothing I read or hear comforts
me— Democracy has brought the South *I fear* into a *sad, sad*
state— Oh that I was in a land free from troubles—but shall
I find that spot— I fear peace & happiness have taken their
flight from this once prosperous land— We forgot our de-
pendence on God—neglected all his appointments & he will
in no wise prosper sinners. Several from the plantation to
day—Mack—Maria—Tena—Phillis, little Sylvia. The two

---

11. According to his biographer, John B. Edmunds, Jr., Pickens was
aloof and overbearing and once wrote that it seemed to be his destiny "to
be disliked by all who know me well." In addition, he had a young wife
(Lucy Petaway Holcombe), a lady clever, pretty, and ambitious, and a
rather inconsistent record on the question of secession. See Edmunds,
Francis W. Pickens and the Politics of Destruction (Chapel Hill, 1986).

first have treated me dreadfully in their time—no one could scarce believe the impudence I have taken from *Mack* & *Maria*— I cannot like them— I will try to treat them as justly as I can—but I have no confidence in them. The others are good negroes, of course I feel very different to them. This was a variable day—cloudy in the morning—brightened about 11 or 12 O'clock—late in the afternoon turned cold.

21st Monday This is a cloudy—cold morning. Mr. Rawlinson sent Hen-
Morning ery out very early to say I could get a good wagon & harness for 150 dollars. I sent Jim with the money & told him to get it for me. Dick came out with the cart—brought a piece of unbleached cotton—the little hand tub—the mended coffee pots— Frank & Hampton helped to drive two cows out— I gave them their breakfast & sent them back. Mrs. Willson sent little Margaret Kitterson to ask me to make a steeple cake for her wedding[12]— I told the child I could not make a *steeple*— I would make her a large cake. Mrs. Willson sent 1 lb. of butter, 2 lb. of brown sugar—2 Doz. eggs & flour to make a *steeple cake*—'twould not be a very lofty one— I have Sylvia at the flour & butter now—hope I may succeed in making a good cake—if I cannot run up a *steeple*— Mrs. Willson is an old fool for marrying a man who has nothing but himself to give her, she will find there are more Ben Willsons than one. My Country my prayer is still with thee!!! Oh that I could do more good.

Tuesday 22 We have had a succession of unpleasant days—but I think this as cold & disagreeable day as any—there is no rain this far, 2 O'clock in the afternoon—but the wind is like ice & the clouds look as if it would as easily snow as rain— I think 'tis too cold to snow— I finished Mrs. Willson's cake[s], one large cake, lb. cake, though it had 1½ lb. of flour, butter, sugar each—eggs &c., &c.,— One lb. of sponge cake, rather a large sponge cake, very near as large as the lb. cake. I only hope she may be as happy as she anticipates being— about one week from this her eyes will be opened to the reality of her folly— I am sent a note asking me to dine with her to day— I declined dining—but promised conditionally to go this afternoon—but the weather forbids—my poor Sister, how often I have thought of you since I received your

12. Probably neighbor Dorcas Wilson who was fifty-five years old.

note yesterday— Often, often do I think of you & pray for you— Oh Lord comfort my dear Sister—*thou canst comfort her*— O hear my prayer if thou dost condescend for the pleadings of one for another:—remember Lord she is the work of *"thine own hands"*— Oh feel for her, if she has neglected her duty to thee, forgive her for Jesus' sake. Now let the prayers of a poor humble servant plead with thee to watch over our soldiers—make them thy children in faith & they will be true to themselves & to their Country. Yesterday Mr. R——— sent out two Cows with young calves. At night—I have seen a little of negro deception to night— I wish the Abolitionists & the negroes had a country to themselves & we who are desirous to practice *truth* & *love to God were to ourselves*—yes, Lord Jesus—separate us in the world to come, let us not be together—it is encouraging to hope liars shall have no part in thee—let the goats be far removed from the sheep— Oh I am sorry when I find out any mean trickery in my servants—our lot is hard to be mixed up with such. Lord forgive me if I judge wrong.

23 Wednesday It commenced sleeting in the night—now every thing is cased in ice—elastic shrubery in some places bent to the ground— I do wish we could see this bad weather pass away & we again see our own dear Southern sunshine. How dreadful this weather is to our poor stock—Cows, sheep & hogs—even the chickens seem to feel the cold—but the foolish geese will be in the sleet—water seems to fascinate a goose— I do believe they would freeze sooner than go under a shelter. With all the ice & rain the wind blows high & did through the night. Pine trees are majestic looking while their limbs are weighed down with ice. The small Peach trees are quite stiff—they do not weep under the load but will sooner break *than bend*. The sugar berry with its long twigs is looking quite graceful. And how are our poor soldiers at the forts & near Charleston fareing through all this? I trust in God our ruling men will see & know they are made comfortable— Let us pray that God is with them & will take care of them— Oh God save our Country from being divided— from being torn asunder to raise up a military government to crush us all— I have little confidence in man— Thou Lord must unite us—must guide us or we are gone—gone— I do wish every son & daughter of Adam was surrounded with as many comforts as I am this day—my servants cannot say they are either cold or hungry—they are all well off— I only wish they knew it—however, there are some spirits that never know this until God strips them of the blessings they possess. I don't say this falsely—I am willing for no Abolitionist to come & say if my throat should be cut by the midnight assassin. Yes, you would say, certainly you have no right to their labour—their labour goes back to them in a great degree—it is not very much we have to waste on luxury—we have to continue buying land to keep them up as well as ourselves—indeed we neat [net] very little. Now four O'clock in the afternoon & we have had a *dreadful* day— it does seem God is angry with us. The ice disappeared rapidly—in an hour after it began to melt all was gone, but the rain pours & the clouds still heavy—though not so angry as they were while it sleeted—in Russia I suppose this would only be a Miatsal [mistral]:—the mildest kind of snow storm—but this has been [a] sleet storm— We have no wingers [winters] here—how thankful we should be for these blessing[s]—if we have ice & snow, nothing suffers where there is feed & protection—of course they suffer but not as those in high Northern latitudes. Had the poultry well fed & they have all gone to seek their roost. I saw Jim a little while ago bring a load of wood for his family—perhaps if he was free he would have to buy this wood—may be have a poor house & a dirt chimney—he has a house—brick fire place with three rooms—one to sit in—two bed rooms.

24th Thursday I was asked by message on tuesday to dine out to day—it is now ten O'clock A.M.—& everything is so wet & the clouds so dreadful in appearance I cannot say whether I shall venture out or not—we have had almost a constant drizzle all the morning & between midnight & day we had a long & pouring rain—the earth must be cushion like in all low places after so much water. I wonder if old Balad will be able to cross the river this day[13]— I hope it is so high he may be disappointed— I am sure it would be better for Mrs. Willson if Old Balad could not reach her to be married—she will be astonished at herself as soon as she realized the fact that she has given up *her child* & *grand children* for a husband— who

---

13. Old Balad may have been an elderly Clarendon District farmer, John W. Ballard. If so, he was not quite so poor as Keziah supposed and owned personal and real property worth about $12,000.

is nothing but a man who wants a home—this I have heard:—that he was entirely dependent, & his relatives were anxious he should get a home. Still cloudy, darker than it was a while ago. Now a thick mist falling. I really will be disappointed if I do not get to Mrs. F. M. Hopkins' to day— where I had hoped to meet other friends. I thank thee Heavenly Father that we are yet spared from civil war. *Lord save our Country!!!* Now night— I have been sadly disappointed not meeting my friends at Fanny's— I love to visit with my friend Fanny, she is ever in good spirits & always has something new about her that she takes great interest in—invariably has a good vegetable garden—she is now very much engaged with her orchards & has a fine variety of trees, I do hope she may succeed & live to enjoy her labour & pleasure, for it really is a pleasure to her to be employed. I am equally fond of viewing God's works in inanimate nature—but am far behind my friend in energy & industry— I do pray for her this prayer, that God may prosper her sons to do well & ere she is much older may send them back to her to minister to her comforts in old age—who knows but one of them may yet be a preacher of the Gospel— What I would give to see one of them, *aye both of them* truely pious & helping up Old Beaulah—Beaulah, I cannot give you up— Lord help me to do more for all good appointments. I felt there was a rebelious spirit in me at one time this day— Lord thou didst help me to put it down. Oh ever be so good as to check these sinful feelings: Thou are good to me, my master—thou hast made me comfortable this night at my own fireside. Lord save our dear Country— Let all stubborn hearts yield to thee & we can yet be one people—if they will not strive to do thy will—they never will succeed in any thing good. Made ginger cakes to day—put only a little butter & a little lard in them. 24—This was a misty day throughout—the sun did not shine a ray this day—sometimes the heavens were lighter, then they would darken—thus the day passed away in hopes & fears.

25 Friday This morning I had high hopes the rain was over— I have not seen the sun to day. This afternoon it is raining very much—there was a very little rain before twelve o'clock— I had Joe moving some trees—he took up two pear trees & planted them again—they had been planted badly—the roots were exposed from shallow planting. Joe has an old apple tree up & will put it in a better place as soon as the rain stops pouring. Oh this gloomy—gloomy weather, it is bad enough to give one the blues— but Christians must drive away such bad company—we must live on hope— I hope our soldiers are comfortable— I do wonder what the S. & the N. are to come to— I pray the strife may soon be ended & let us all resolve to be obedient to God's will, but die sooner than submit to what is wrong. It is hard for one who knows little of diplomacy to know what man is aiming at— all pretend to be patriots—& we have a right to suspect one party wants the loaves & fishes as well as the other—Democrats—republicans—whigs or federalists. I hope the South will shew herself honourable through this strife— God will not prosper her if she is deceptive. Lord save us, thy poor children.

Saturday 26th The rain is pouring this morning—the Heavens are lighter at this moment—still raining hard & the yard has been sheeted with water—last night & is now—strange weather—I hope our soldiers are comfortable. I begin to fear I have a cancer on the right side of my neck inwardly— I suffered very much awhile last night. I certainly ought to be ready to die when My God pleases to take me—he has kindly tried to wean me from earth—left me no strong ties to come between us—if I am not prepared & willing to meet my God—who can be— Oh Lord help me to do thy will— I am blest in worldly things—still I am often fretted by these *very things*—have mercy on me & teach me to love thee so I may count all things here as dust—too worthless to fret about— I have some good negroes & I wish them well— I pray God will place them in good places when I am taken from them— I have others who seem to dislike me & never care to look at me—such I hope may one day know they were well to be under my care— I don't wish them very bad luck— I only wish them to feel they are no better than other servants—with me they are proped up by a large family & presume on it by making others succumb to them—these are the ones I hope may be made to feel that power is not *always* to the strong—yes if all were freed in a day—these very families would enslave the small families. Negroes are strange creatures— I cannot tell whether they have any good feelings for their owners or not—sometimes I think they have—then I think their is nothing but deception in them—

I am heartily tired of managing them—could I cast them off without scruples of conscience—I would do so as soon as we can have peace—but I have thought all this over seriously, I cannot do it & feel that I have done right—they have been with us & our forefathers two generations back—have worked for us & contributed to our comforts & could I for a misdemeanor now & then cast them off without a rebuke from my Heavenly father—while I believe I am an accountable being I cannot do it. Lord help me to patience while on earth— Precisely 8 m. before 12 O'clock the sun shone out a few seconds—he is again hidden behind the thick clouds— I do hope ere he goes down the dark clouds will wind far away & let us once more be cheered by glamorous *Sol*.

27 Sunday I am thankful God put it into my heart to go to church this day— This was the first bright day we had had in a long time—indeed I cannot tell when the sun has been as bright as it was this day—still not a beautiful day. Emma persuaded me to go home with her from church. I remained all night—Mr. Edward Gunter was there.[14] A Professor Smith preached at Beaulah on this day—he is from Louisville, Kentucky—what on earth brought him this way I cannot tell— I confess I am always suspicious of persons who roam about with some thing to effect by it— I ought not to indulge in such thoughts.

28 Monday Left Emma's after breakfast—came to the plantation—after dinner left—came to Sister's, spent an hour with her, then came back home. This was a beautiful pleasant day—

29th We have a bright morning—the wind is quite piercing cold & blowing strong—it matters not how God frowns on us from the elements, we feel we can submit to it—there seems to be mercy in it in some way—but when it is through man, we shudder—& why? because we feel man has so much of *Satan's spirit in him:*—unless renewed by God man is a very *Devil*—this is true & all who study mankind will know it— I never think seriously on this but I feel very bad— I am so thankful for all God's mercies— What is the South contend-

---

14. In the early nineteenth century, the Gunter family owned a farm on Back Swamp that later became the property of James and English Hopkins. Edward Gunter (age thirty-five in 1850, no occupation) is not listed in the 1860 census.

ing for—she is or has to work against a set of fanatics—who would glory in shedding every drop of white blood—for what & why she has encouraged such feelings?—it must be because in place of serving God in the way *we are commanded*—they have just lived on the hope of reaping all we have by & through their lying ways. If we were cut off they might come in & usurp our power in a way that might sound better—but which in the end will crush our slaves out of the country or this world. Growing colder, I am really glad I did not go to the mill this morning. Lord remember those who are exposed for our safety & have mercy on us all. At night—my arm is paining me dreadfully—& my corns seem to try themselves. This day Ned & John finished throwing down the corn beds.

Wednesday 30 Oh my God I see nothing ahead but trouble— Our country will pass from bad to worse—the South never would be united or it might have sent Douglass instead of Lincoln—if she could have been united 'twould have been far better for her— I do hope if we have Civil war—that God will take me before the first drop of blood is shed— O God canst thou, wilt thou not spare us— I do not say we deserve it—no—no—slavery ever will make trouble I care not where found— I wish I had been born without them with a sufficiency to keep me from want in as good a country as this with our liberal religion— My God!! My God!!—save us from wars within— Oh our negroes, how much we have to bear with from them— I have some I scarce ever get a civil word from no matter how kind & indulgent to them. This is *a most beautiful day*—though the wind is rather high. Sylvia, if slavery continues I hope no relative I have will keep you about them—nothing on this earth can change your heart—it is a *bad one*— The truth is, Sylvia *hates* a white face— I firmly believe this from the conduct of her whole life. Lord, if I judge wrong, forgive me— Wednesday in the afternoon I went down to Cabin branch, staid all night.

31 Thursday This is a cool morning—but a fine bright day for my ride to Columbia— I went up to see Handy—saw Dr Huo to day.[15] While up got oats—ten bushels for the Sand Hills at 80

---

15. Handy, one of Keziah's slaves, was being treated by Dr. Huot. Her domestic notes reveal she loaned Handy clothing and blankets that were to be returned when she recovered.

cts.—paid Mrs. Scott's bill of 13.71 cts.— Mrs. Scott did not date her bill, which she certainly ought to have done— got shoes from Olivers' for Jim & Sylvia—paid 2.75 for the two pair—Oranges 50 cts.—Garden seed 40 cts.—gave Mary one dollar & Margia 50 cts.—left her coffee, rice & some sausages—this visit I have not spent money foolishly— got back to Cabin branch at night[16]—

16. Mrs. Nancy Scott was a Columbia dressmaker, and John and Alexander Oliver sold boots and shoes at 197 Richardson Street. Mary and Margia appear to have been slaves who maintained Keziah's city home at Bull and Blanding streets.

February
"The deception of my servants disheartens me."

Friday 1st   We have a misty morning for the 1st of February—this is not a cold day— I hope the month will not be warm enough to put the trees to blooming—sometimes Feb. is a sad month on our hopes for fruit, there comes a mild time—the trees bloom out & are sure to be injured by March winds. I see a little sunshine at present now between 12 & 1 O'clock & the wind is rising— Yesterday evening cannons were fired in Col———, what for I know not— I hope all things may settle down for the good of the human family the world over. I am not in a good or bad frame of mind this morning— I feel careless— Lord help me to holy feelings—make me love *thee* more & more for Oh I mourn this indifference—would I not be better in heart if I had no slaves? This is hard to answer— God has given them to us— Now Lord, help us to do right with them. Late in the afternoon—still cloudy & drizzly. I have sinned this day grumbling with my poor negroes, I ought to have more patience. 'Tis now late & raining hard.

2nd Saturday   The morning mild but cloudy— I saw two trees planted that came from my lot in Columbia & a cherry tree taken out of the garden & planted in the front lawn—had a rose & a small shrub & a small golden Bell [Forsythia] put out—after two o'clock it commenced raining & we have had a great deal of rain this afternoon—the yard was sheeted with water in a few minutes—now just dark—raining still, moderately. Just read Dr Thornwell's sermon delivered on thanksgiving day—it is decidedly the best one I have read—he spoke as a christian should have done— I mean his sentiments were those of a christian through out. I read it in the Southern Presbyterian review.[1] I dislike to read any thing about the

---

1. Thornwell's sermon, "National Sins—A Fast-Day Sermon preached in the Presbyterian Church, Columbia, Wednesday, November 21, 1860," appeared in the *Review* (January 1861), pp. 649–88. With minor reservations, it was a ringing endorsement of the Confederate cause.

present crisis—we have nothing to hope for from man & as a nation we are obliged to say we have sinned with a high hand & as individuals we are a vain & conceited people—we who profess to be disciples of Christ—have none of his spirit. Lord help us. This day I received a letter from my Dear Sister Peggy Brevard—she mentioned the death of her brother— I have ever had an exalted opinion of Mr. Conner—when I heard of his death I felt Charleston had lost one of her purest characters.[2] I wept over Sister's letter— I wish I had language to tell her how I sympathised with her— Mr. Conner is a loss to the community— When such men thought our South was wronged it was a consolation to me— I feared our State acted too hastily & perhaps had better watched over herself & borne a little longer sooner than break up this government so soon, perhaps ere all who had strugeled for her independence had gone home to their God. Mr. Conner's father & one, perhaps two brothers—one I am sure fought for our independence—they were born in Ireland & I have heard No. Carolinians remark what handsome, fine looking men the Conners were—when young men. The Conners were Protestants—Presbyterians in No. Ca——— I have heard nothing could rouse Old Mr. James Conner more than add the O to his name—it savored of Rome too much for that friend of liberty.

3rd of February It rained very much last night & has been raining all this morning. This is a wet, wet day—not cold— I wish I was in Heaven away from this *mean, deceitful, lying* world—there is nothing here to encourage a good thought but the promises of the Saviour—if we were not encouraged by his word we would be a world of disponding wretches— Oh my God help thy dear children from these *low grounds*— Oh help, help!! help us up—help us up—the deception of my servants disheartens me— Oh it almost makes me hate them when I find out their feelings to me—with all I have done for them—they seem at times to hate me as though I had satan's principles in me—all I can plead is Lord forgive me & Oh take me from this world to a better—it has been my constant desire to make my negroes happy—& I am every now & then awakened to the fact that they *hate me*— My God— My

---

2. Henry Conner, age sixty-four, former president of the Bank of South Carolina and the South Carolina Rail Road, died on 11 January 1861.

God—what are we to expect from slaves—when mine hate me as they do—it is nothing on earth—but that I am *white* & own slaves— My Southern Sisters & brothers who think their slaves would be on our side in a civil war, will, I fear, find they have been artfully taken in— I did not believe I had negroes who would use such language towards me as I have heard Sylvia & Dick used— I have ever disliked Sylvia & I begin to think very different of Dick—to what I once did, I had a better opinion of him, he is a member of the methodist church, I may judge him wrong—his countenance is very savage like.

4 Monday We had a pouring rain last evening & it continued to pour till after midnight— I really felt uneasy about so much water on & in the earth—the yard was sheeted with water— This morning still very cloudy— My arm still painful. I spent yesterday bad, indulging in sinful feelings all day—every time I woke in the night I prayed to God to help me to a better frame of mind to day— My God check me from sin & let me act like a rational christian— I know I indulge or rather do not strive against sin as I should— I live too far from God & mourn my lukewarmness. Forgive me Lord—& make me one of thy humble servants. *Oh My God save* our dear—dear Country!!! Let our soldiers be converted to be true christians—they now have leisure to dwell on thee, to pray to *thee* & ask of thee all that is worth having in this world:—religion—the religion of our blessed Lord & Master. Give to our rulers Oh *God* firmness in all that is good & right in thy sight.

Tuesday 5th The sun is shining now between eleven & twelve O'clock— This is cheering— I wish I could forsee when our country's prospects would cheer up & let us go to work with hopes of peace & happiness. I have been angry & spoken my mind freely this morning. I have to take impudence & when I think of of it, it makes me give way to very *ill* feelings & another thing is it makes me judge uncharitably. At night. I believe the sun went down clear of cloud.

Wednesday 6th This was a beautiful day, the sun shined like silver. I had the gobbler hashed for dinner to day. New ham fried with eggs—old ham boiled that came out on the 21st of January—rice—Coffee—Pan cakes & egg custard for dinner. Mr. & Mrs. Rawlinson were out. I was sick in bed all day— did not see Mr. R——— but he sent by Mrs. R——— 42 dollars he had received for ginning R. Spigner's cotton & 5.25 left of the money I gave him to pay the negroes for their corn—their corn brought them 220 dollars— I took it & gave them 90 cts. per bushel. In the afternoon Amy & Sally Hopkins came & staid awhile.

7th Thursday Another bright day— I remained in bed this day. This is the day that Jim got so insulted because I sent word for Sam to work with John—instead of coming to me & asking me not to let Sam & John be together, he gave John a kick in the stomache, a severe one—the boy came to me crying— No other servant in this yard but *Jim or one of his family would have risked such an insult to me*— Jim is an impudent negro—& every servant knuckels to him—if they do not—his family will put them down— I intend to tell this to James H. Adams— if one of the others had treated me thus they would be punished & why not Jim— I have taken impudence unmeasured from his four daughters—Sylvia—Tama—Mack—Maria— If it is so ordered that any of these fall to my nieces & nephews, I pray you sell them & let not your white family be ran over by such ungovernable people—

Friday 8th Another bright day— Oh that man could appreciate these blessings— I hope our soldiers are over the worst of the winter— Lord Jesus take care of them—intercede for their souls. Mary is this day preparing a bed for small seed, Tom working with her. Friday 8th I put up $2.25 in Silver in Mrs. Bunche's right pocket—some in paper.[3]

9 Saturday Sun shines to day—not so bright as it has done— some cloud—by tomorrow we will be apt to have another change. Jim begins to cave in a little— Jim is a self willed negro & wants every servant on the place to look to him as a superior & he has had great influence over my negroes. I hope his power is on the wane— I think him very cautious in his moves & determined too— I may judge him wrong—but why is it his family have always been so impudent to me— they must be encouraged by Mamy or Dady on— Dolly is as stubborn as an ox & her example has given me great trouble— I wish their hearts could be changed.

---

3. The meaning of this statement is unclear, but it may be a private joke meaning Keziah "squirreled away" some money for future use. No census indicates a Mrs. Bunche was living in the neighborhood, and it was unlike Keziah to give money quite so freely.

Sunday 10th This is a cloudy windy day—no rain yet—it will rain, I think. My arm is not very painful— I am not well enough to go to church to day— Lord help me spend this day right. The day has past—forever gone—still with Jobe I must say I will trust in God though he slay— I cannot live without my God. This Holy day I received a letter from Harriet Russell & a note from Jane M. Adams senior.

Monday 11th This has been a wet day—raining constantly—no ploughing done this day— Joe & Dick put out some quinces & peaches—balance cutting & marking rails. I wish I could see some intelligent person to tell me something about the state of our country. I am sorry to hear of the distress in Kansas[4]— Oh God save the people & give them right hearts—if any arrangement is made to help them I will add my mite— I pray they may receive help from us—

12 Tuesday I thank thee Heavenly Father for thy protection through the night—& for this beautiful smiling morn. The sun is bright, the earth cushioned with water— I hope this genial season will not bring forth blooms—'tis too early yet. I am affraid I neglect my bees— I know so little about manageing them. I would like to see Fanny & ask her all about it. Now I am in the spirit I ought to answer Harriet's cheerful letter— I am seldom cheerful myself.

Wednesday 13th Another lovely bright day— I wish my heart corresponded with this day—but ever since *Jim's dareing* impudence to me—when he kicked John for delivering my message—I am not satisfied— I do not think I ought to let it pass without punishment— I never did have such impudence offered me— I am determined to tell James H. of it—& let him act on it—I have always thought Jim was deep in his maneuvers—cautious & cowardly— & I think would be a dangerous negro if not rightly managed—it is seldom he shews this daring impudence—yet you can see he thinks himself right in every case where he is implicated—yet at times seems to mean right—it is hard to fathom a *real rascal*—if I judge Jim wrong I pray to be forgiven— I have raised four of his daughters—every one has been just as impudent as they desired to be—whipping did very little good & good treatment made them think themselves better than white people—& poor Dolly she has ever been a miserable woman—too

---

4. Keziah is referring to the struggle in that state over slavery.

proud & ignorant— she never would go to church unless as fine & fashionable as possible. Now she sits & does nothing, too contrary almost to live—the Lord punishes those who are not thankful for mercies— I think Dolly has been very ungrateful— Lord forgive me if I judge my poor negroes wrong— I feel sorry they are slaves— I know I treat *them* far better than they treat me— I am attached to those who do well—but they care nothing for me— *self is all.*

14th Thursday Mary returned from Col———, brought a Hat for Tom— Shoes for myself—knitting needles for Dorcas—gave Mary 3.00—returned 50 cts.— This is a cloudy day, the wind is high— this day I feel more sadly about my country than I have for several weeks— I see nothing but trouble before us. Oh my God what shall I pray? & how shall I pray? Spare us good Lord! spare us!! The evening of this day my good friend Mrs. Jones came— I was truely rejoiced to see her— soon after she got here we had quite a hard shower of rain.

Friday 15 This morning a few passing clouds—but the wind rose— blew high all day & the sun shined brightly—it was a pretty bright day to the eye—the wind rendered it a disagreeable day out doors. My friend remained with me through this day & I really enjoyed her society.

16 This is a beautiful morning. How changing are all things— soon after breakfast it got quite cloudy—about 11 A.M.—a shower—then the wind blue almost a storm the balance of this day— Now after dark the stars are out & 'tis quite cold— Mrs. Jones left soon after breakfast, I hope she got home before the wind blew so high— While Mrs. J———s was with me—had a New Ham, a Young Gobler, one of Miss Mary's, & one fowl. The ham used this time was the last new ham brought out— I had had a few slices fried off it the day Mr. & Mrs. Rawlinson were out.

Sunday Before breakfast. O my God—I thank thee for taking care of me through the night, I thank thee for guarding my Coun- try—Lord we are not worthy—but on thy intercession is our *whole trust*—save us all to the end & redeem this world entire from Satan's power—watch over us, & help us up from ev- ery sin—they so easily beset frail human nature:—without thy aid blessed Jesus we should despair. This is a cold, clear bright morning. I do hope the wind may not rise to day. I fear yesterday's ride may make Mrs. Jones sick—the wind was *powerful*—her carriage had no curtain in the front. The wind did rise to day but not like yesterday & it became quite cloudy before sun down. This has been a cold day through out.

18th Monday Emma came to day— I had a young rooster baked for dinner—Sausages & Eggs fried—pan cakes—used seven eggs this day. This is a cold, cloudy day—disagreeable to feel & to look on— Harry & Mary have left to go to Col. to Dr Fair & H——— tomorrow.[5] I pray all may happen for the best— *Lord help us all.* Yesterday was sunday— I did not spend the day as I wished or should have done. I fear this cold will injure the oats that is in the ground— I have at least eighty bushels sown—hoping to help out the corn crop of last year. This is the first visit Emma ever made me comeing entirely alone—it seems strange—she looked lonely coming out of her carriage entirely alone— Amy in Columbia & Sally going to school at Fanny Hopkins' to Miss Service.[6] I sent English two bottles of hom[e]made wine & gave Emma one— gave Emma some Artichokes in Salt & water for pickeling & some Cucumber pickels. This day had only part of a cold ham on the table. Lent Emma two jars to be returned. (These returned.)

Tuesday 19th This was a gloomy looking morn, now 11 O'clock—the sun shines dimly & a great deal of smoke around— I suppose from clearings in the neighbourhood— Yesterday Emma insisted I should go over this evening—this day is so cold I feel very reluctant to leave home. Have I forgotten to thank my God for saving our country?— I hope not— Lord fit me for a better world— I pray I may not live to see my country involved in a civil war. Oh my God make me willing to give up every thing on this earth— I ought not to wish to look back—what have I to turn for—is there any thing on this earth to induce me to do so—have I not lived to see—all is "vanity & vexation of *spirit*"—if we do no good here there is nothing to live for.

20 Wednesday This is a bright morning—the weather tolerably mild. Sun shines tolerably bright. I feel my rebellious spirit rise this

---

5. Mary, a slave, was being treated at the clinic maintained by Fair & Huot.

6. Fanny Tucker Hopkins established "Magnolia School" in the basement of her home for her grandchildren, classes that were attended by other young people as well.

morning— I promised to go to Emma's—every time I think of Jim's impudence—my spirit boils—so I feel I hate he should ever drive me again—if I were to shew my feelings they would only *devil* me the more— I am one who has ever been willing there should be a plan devised to get negroes out of our beautiful country & this institution in our midst has greatly reconciled me to my lot—lonely as some suppose—while I know if troubles come I have no children to meet it—I am satisfied the Lord has been good to me. If I had had children I have always said I would have tried to get them away from negro slavery—am I right or am I wrong— God's ways must be right—he has put them here for some wise purpose & I know I should leave all in his hands & not murmur as I do—but it is hard for a poor, lonely female to take impudence— I have taken gross impudence hundreds of times & let it pass unpunished—this would not hurt me as it does if I was indifferent to them—but I am constantly administering to their comforts & do it literally—let any one look over my annual accounts & I feel proud to know it— I have never looked on them as beasts of burden—working for my pleasure—I think I am responsible for all I do for them & to them. I am reading Motley['s] Dutch Republic[7]— Oh my God a wretch man is without the restraints of the pure religion of our blessed Saviour— Many things have been done under the name of the religion of Jesus Christ, but Christ had no part in the religion of Charles V & Philip the second of Spain—why such wretches were permitted to deluge nations in blood—man cannot answer—but God thou knowest the depravity of the human heart & thou didst desire to shew to the world what was pure & holy & what was detestable to *thee*—perhaps it required all this to shew "who were thy peculiar people zealous of good works"—for this thou didst suffer—& I pray thy good work is growing on & will continue growing till thy knowledge shall crush Satan from this *earth*— Hasten the day when the kingdom shall come. Wednesday evening—I went to Cabin branch, thence to Emma's—

---

7. John Lothrop Motley's *Rise of the Dutch Republic* first appeared in 1836, and in the late 1850s his two-volume *History of the United Netherlands* was published. The latter was being advertised by a Columbia store in 1860, so this may have been what Keziah was reading.

21st Spent this day with Emma— Cousin W^m went to the sale at Mr. Roache's—bid on the land for David— Ben Spigner got the Hayly piece & Mr. Roach got the home tract[8]— This evening Amy came down with David & Ada— Wm Martin, son of the Revd Wm Martin, died at 3 O'clock this morning at the Female College in Columbia So. Ca.—is to be buried at 10 tomorrow in the Washington Street Methodist Churchyard.[9] The 20 and 21st were good dry days with sunshine—there is so much smoke it almost dims the sunshine.

Friday 22 This is a fine morning—the wind blows every day— I hope Feb. will take all the boisterous winds to herself & let us have a calmer March. I left Emma's after breakfast— They had two fine shad for breakfast— Now one o'clock P.M. & I am at my Sand Hill home. This Morning's papers give us no encouragement— I fear Lincoln's administration will be a dire one to *the South*. Lord help us—for we can do nothing of ourselves. 22 Sylvia said to me tonight—"*Dr Ray was no body, no how.*" This is the way negroes talk in these days. These were her very words.

Saturday 23rd This has been a tolerably pleasant day—the wind high—in the afternoon an occasional sprinkling—had Irish potatoes planted—the large square enriched with bags of hair—the small—from the stable & old garden— This day had lime slacked & dissolved in water, then sprinkled the floors of my fowl houses, coops, &c., &c.—up at the house—sprinkled lime before the South door of the kitchen— I thank *thee* Heavenly Father for thy protection & kindness to me through this day—thou has guarded me from the anger & vexation I am often beset with— Oh that I could keep this in mind & serve thee better—but Heavenly Father I can do nothing of myself:—any good & perfect gift is from thee. *Oh my God* save our country from war & make the No. & the So. bow to thee as thy humble servants—*we are thine, wholy thine* & thou ca[n]st *do with us as it pleases thee*. Money. When I called at the plantation on Wednesday the 20th I left with Mrs. Rawlinson three ten dollar bills & one two dollar bill to pay

---

8. This sale consisted of two pieces of land (130 and 250 acres) that bordered on Keziah's property, hence her interest in these transactions.

9. The elder Martin became president of what is now Columbia College in 1860. The son, who had contracted typhoid while stationed at Fort Moultrie, was saluted by his father with these words: "The first Martyr to Southern Independence. . . . Alas poor child."

Mr. Beck's bill & get some pea seed & Onion Setts.[10]
KGBH . . . 1861.

Sunday 24th 'Twas cloudy & warm early—now between 2 & 3 P.M. clear
& windy—the wind cold. Psalm VI—O Lord rebuke not in
thine anger, neither chasten me in thy hot displeasure. 2nd
V[erse] Have mercy on me O Lord, for *I am weak:* O Lord,
heal me for my bones are vexed. I thank thee merciful Father
for making this rebellious spirit yield to thee this day—how
can I repay thee for *this one help*—much less for the hourly
blessings, I am debtor to thee—

25 A bright cold morning wind blowing. I expect to go to the
mill to day. I have almost lost all desire to do for my servants—they treat me so mean & very much to suit themselves—all my kindness & liberality to them is as so much
ill—they take every thing as for self interest. 25—I went to
the mill—got there after one O'clock—left between 3 & 4
pass[ed] the R.R.—going & comeing near the time for the
train to pass—did not see or hear it—lucky. Gabriel sick at
the mill—so was Lalla, yet I never thought of Lalla— I am
sorry I forgot her— I have so many things to think off—this
is no excuse for my neglect.

26 I staid at Cabin branch last night—came home to the
Sand Hills this morning—true my feelings are in a better state—the grief to me is that I cannot control my feelings— Unworthy I know I am—but shame on me that I
cannot soar above such lamintations [limitations?]— I think
when I am mourning thus of the Quaker & the Methodist—
the M———— pouring out his doleful case in prayer, the
Q———— thought if he was such a sinner he should leave
him—said, Friend if thou art such a sinner I will leave
thee to thyself— Yesterday was a fine cold day— This day
has been rather warm, now at night 'tis quite cloudy. Now
near 8 O'clock—little Ben has brought the Shad out—
Mr. R———— got them from the Col———— ice house to day.
Sausages— Left in the new house this morning 180 links of
Sausages—gave Mrs. R———— 32 links & brought 46 to
Sand Hills—now 180 left. I miss ten links of sausages.

---

10. Charles Beck was a well-to-do Columbia carpenter who operated a
sash-blind factory. Keziah probably owed him for materials used by
Tom Prescott during construction and repair at her mill place.

27th This is a dim morning. Rosanna said this morning she wished she could leave me & never look behind at me again— I only wish she could get *her* wish— I don't wish any one about me who has no good feelings for me. I don't wish her any greater ill than to go away from me. 27th— Mrs. Adams was to see me to day—she was owing me $5.12 cts. for wheat & Rye— Mrs. A. paid me two dollars in cash to day—Mrs. A——— says I got 6 ½ doz. eggs from her in the fall & Christmast at 15 cts. which makes 1.05 cash— 2.00—1.05 makes 3.05 paid—the balance still due 2.07 cts.

28th This is a beautiful morning— I love such a bright day, but I fear the charming temperature will bring forth vegetation only to be sniped by the cold march winds. Now what of my country?—a few short days & we shall hear from Lincoln's lips what we may expect—if he makes war on us the whole body of men No. & So. should rise against him & make a blow at the man himself who would dare to bring such trouble on this land won by the blood of our fore fathers from British encroachments. If the N. should be let loose on us, the fanatics will run mad with joy & tongues cannot tell where the scene will end—if ever, until a dark age sinks the nation into brutes— I consider the vast body of our slaves little above brutes— I am sorry to think it—*but I be- lieve it*. Many white faces in this land of light sin high in the presence of God sitting our poor negroes degraded examples— I thank the Heavenly Father I have never had a son to mix my blood with *negro* blood— Oh such a sin would [be] & is disheartening to Christian Mothers— Lord be with Christians every where—not christians in *name*—but those who love thy ways & try to follow Christ's example while on earth— I mean to live & do good & sin not—& set pure exalted examples as he did while on earth—Cash. I this day have in cash 62 dollars— I owe for the press—2 tables—1 box & repairing 4 windows— I think 17 or 18 dollars—must be paid out of the 62 dollars—'twill soon be gone.

[Here a portion of the text is heavily scribbled over.]

I went out to day & some of my mean little negroes scribbled over this—sometimes I think Sylvia did it to make me whip Dorcas. *Lord Jesus*— Save our dear country from war.

March
"Punish us, but not by civil war."

Friday 1st day of March just before day it seemed to me I felt the earth vibrate frequently as though cannons were booming in the distance— Oh Lord what is to be our fate. This morning Jane & her daughter Laura called to see me, I was rejoiced to see them & hear from the family. This is an uncommon warm day— I have been out & had my fowl houses attended to—nests scalded—old straw burnt & new put in—ashes strewn over the nests & floors. This evening I hope to look over my young Apple trees— O my master save our Country *from war & bloodshed*. In eight days I will be fifty eight years old. If I had been a useful woman these many years what a happiness 'twould be to take a retrospect of them— I cannot see what I have done to any one or in any cause to make me feel I have been useful in my generation—blessed be the Lord that *my all* depends on him & through him. This is a calm evening—some thing soothing in the appearance & feeling of all around. Would that we were once more a quiet nation— perhaps these troubles we are in may be blessed to us.

March 2nd Sunshines—a pleasant day—a great deal of smoke. I put half a bushel of guano on a square— I intend transplanting my first cabbage plants—the large york. We have a little wind to day—none yesterday— I hope March may not be a stormy month—we had a bad Jan——y & Feb.—this March comes in very mild. Let Sister's Matilda have half a bushel of homney this morning. Now bed time— I sent Ned off early this morning to meet Mary, thinking she was at Cabin Branch place—he has not returned— I do not know what to think of it. I hope nothing serious has kept him. This is a really warm night. The fruit trees are blooming out rapidly, a few more such days every peach tree & plum will be in full bloom & those now out will be over. This dividing & splitting up our union I fear is to be our end as a people— I do mourn over it & can't help feeling we are undone—undone— Oh my God help us—fit us for Heaven & take us to our lasting home where the weary shall be forever at rest &

the wicked have no chance of disturbing them. Oh God, hear the prayer of all who plead for this dear land of ours. Monday will be the fourth of March [Lincoln's inaugural]— Lord! Lord! what is our doom?

March 3rd This is a march day—blowing earnestly— Heard this morning of Bell Gracey's death[1]—she is far better off than we who are left:—no more sin, no more sorrow for her. Received a note from J. M. A———— to day[2]—saying James H. was very complaining & Laura had sore throat— I heard yesterday Mary A. Kitterson was very ill—they had sent for the D^r— I hope the sore throat is not in the Sand Hills, & hope most may soon be better.

Monday 4th This morning is a little cloudy. I hope it may rain this day— I pray that Lincoln's administration may disappoint his friends & his opposers—his friends are black republicans, our enemies—they must have dreadful hearts to wish to cut our throats because we are sinners—as if they were pure & undefiled—no surer sign of what deceivers they are than to see how self conceited they are— God can punish every sinner & will do it—perhaps many of them may yet have their eyes opened to the enormity of *their own* sins—if not in this world in the next. Blessed be the Lord God Almighty who will make each answer for their own sins—& this will be like millstones to many deceivers. Thankful I am that I have a just God to go before & not Northern fanatics nor black Republicans— Lord let me have right feelings towards them because it [is] thy will, we should forgive our enemies. 'Tis hard for us to feel right towards those who sent John Brown (that Devil) to cut our throats— Now Oh my God remember this *nation in Mercy*—spare us good lord & help us to do thy *will*. Tom Prescott has been out & given me a bill to finish the old smoke house. I paid Tom all I owed him—we are now balanced in money—paid him twenty one dollars for making a press, two tables & one box—too much I know, he charged double what I expected to pay for the tables. Now about 8 O'clock at night— I was very angry a little while this afternoon—it seems like mocking my maker to beg so

1. The funeral of Isabel W. Gracey (born 1839), daughter of dry goods merchant John I. Gracey, was held at Columbia's Presbyterian Church at "3½ o'clock" on 2 March.
2. Jane Margaret Adams, wife of James Hopkins Adams.

earnestly one hour for help to do better then so soon to let *sin master me*. Lord thou art our maker— Oh what a blessed thought!! thou wilt help thy children, let me not presume on thy goodness—but trust in thee for help.

March 5th
Tuesday
The wind is very high this bright day. Now 9 O'clock at night & a very great change since last night—'tis now axtrimely cold—the stars all bright. Appearances of fire this evening—great smoke & the high wind, I feel anxious about it. Do hope & pray no one has been in trouble this day from fire—or any other bad element.

6th of March
A cold day—clear day. Mrs. T. Munson here to day.[3] I gave her flannel for two frocks for her child & nearly one peck of I[rish] potatoes.

Thursday 7th
I spent this day at J. H. A. & called to see Mrs. F. M. H. & Miss Service. No one can tell me what Mr. Lincoln intends towards the South— I trust God will say "peace be still"— *his* word will prevail no matter what L. & Seward desire.

Friday 8th
This is a piercing cold morning—now after Mid day—the sun shines brightly. I rather think there is a little change— I am in the house, cannot judge very well.

Saturday 9th
This is a dreadful windy day, but [sun] shining brightly all day—last night a good deal of rain fell.— I had some burning in the new ground early, but was cautious & had the fires put out before the hands came to their dinners— Now clear, bright & the wind very high, 4 O['clock] A.M. I gave my Cook some cold turkey to make a little soup for my dinner— I tired waiting for it—at last said something about my soup—she had made it & given it to Dolly & Mary, said she understood me 'twas for them— I scolded & I got impudence in turn—she kept telling me—she wished I would send her to Mr. B. Brevard[4]—said before she would eat any thing she cooked for me again she would starve— Rosanna never got the first particle of my dinner— 'tis now late in the afternoon—no body knows the impudence I take here almost weekly— I do hope my sausy negroes may get where they will stand in fear when they are done with me.

---

3. Wife of thirty-two-year-old Thomas Munson, a local mechanic.
4. Robert ("Bob") Brevard, Keziah's brother-in-law, who carried on his father's iron business in Lincoln County, North Carolina. He died in 1879 at the age of eighty.

Sunday Morning Lord make me spend this day to thy glory. Jim, Rosanna &
10th of March John got papers to go to Beaulah Church. Sunday a bright,
cold, windy day—very unpleasant indeed.

Monday 11th This is a bright, cold morning—my flour is out, I must
open another bag this day. The bag lasted from the 1st day
of January 1861 to this 11th day of March 1861—out of this
I gave a bucket (full at the mill) for the sick at the mill—for
sick in Col————one for Dolly—near one for Mary— every now & then a pint to different ones— I am satisfied this
has been justly dealt with. I found the lock left open once.
Let me *here—now & forever thank God for his protecting kindness.*

Tuesday 12th This has been a fine day—I went to Sister's after I took my
dinner—she is not well—her foot and ankle inflamed—she
scarce knows the cause—thinks she struck the rocker of her
chair—then went out & stood a good long while in the cold
on it—it is almost purple—poor dear Sister, how I do feel
for you—but *God* is good & he may send you comfort that
we no [sic] not of— Lord be with her—with me—& with all
thy dependent children—for thou art our only help in sorrow & trouble. Frank & Munson came out yesterday to get
posts for a garden— Frank came yesterday— Munson this
morning.

Wed. 13th A fine pleasant day—walked to Jim Gray's field[5]—at home
by 11 A.M. I cannot tell how I spent this day—churned to
day.

Thursday 14th I went to the mill—a little cloudy in the morning—weather
quite mild—while at the mill I heard several distant thunder,
quite loud—left the mill after 3 O'clock—when I got to the
R. R. I became alarmed, the clouds looked so dark I feared
a spring storm—when I reached Mr. Lykes' opening "hope
revived," my fears dispelled & I reached the plantation just
as the rain began to drop from the exhausted cloud[6]—
remained all night. It rained in the night & the wind blew
very high.

Friday 15th This was a dreadful looking morning— The wind very
strong—cold & cloudy— I left Dorcas & came home knowing all things would fare better by my being here. 'Tis now

---

5. Jim Gray, a nearby planter who was forty-three years old in 1850, is
not cited in the 1860 census.
6. Jesse Lykes, age forty-five, a local farmer whose family gave their
name to Lykesland.

5 m[inutes] of 12 O'clock & have some hopes of its clearing off by night—certainly this is a cold—cold day—we have had a few mild days—this disappoints our hopes on the garden & the fruit. Thursday night Mr. R—— gave me all the papers & accounted for 140 dollars given him—paid all I expected & gave me a balance of 7.65 cts.— I left with him this morning 15 dollars to get oil, Turpentine, salts—beef—pay Mrs. McKenzie & some other things[7]—thus goes the money—at the end of the year I fear there will be little left.

16 Saturday Before I went to bed last night every star was *unusually bright* & this briliant morning makes me forget yester morn— This is a cold morning— I fear Friday's cold wind on the rain of the night before may have ruined our fruit—we cannot tell for some time if it has done so. Let me here thank my Heavenly Father for spareing this dear land from war & bloodshed— Oh God preserve us to the end & make us all thy true followers—let us all try to do good & be contented with our lot here on earth— *"Cleanse thou me"* is my prayer *now* & *Oh may it ever be.*

Sunday 17th This is a hazy looking day— Jane wrote a note saying her mother was sick & Amy Hopkins had had sore throat. I thought it strange Emma had not been to see me. My arm seems to be improving gradually.

18th Monday This has been a cold wet day— I fear some of my little chickens will freeze this night— My feelings are not good to day— I have heard of fighting on my place & I am not satisfied that some negroes should be punished every time they fight & others go unpunished. I think Jim's family & Old Dick's descendants are enough to kill any one who thinks to manage them. I begin to see that Ben wants to do as he pleases— Old Dick's & Old Jacob's descendants are next high in power & the ruling spirits at Cabin branch. I just want to hear that our blessed country is safe—then I want to get rid of all my bad negroes— I want to spend my last day quietly. Lord give me firmness to do what is right. *Oh my God save us all.* Near 9 o'clock at night—nature takes strange freaks some would say— This afternoon it commenced freezing— now it is snowing— I can see the tops of the houses are white & the steps—how sorry I am to see & feel

---

7. Mrs. McKenzie cannot be identified, although in 1860 several families bearing that name lived in adjoining Sumter District.

this weather— I see no chance to save the peaches. God can do all things & we must not murmur—but feel thankful he gives food & raiment to keep us from sufferings. Oh God preserve us from war & let us know that this cold is a trifle compared to what thou couldst send on us— I have ventured to read a little to day— I do not see any thing very encouraging— Lord save us—we are not worthy—but spare us & make us better. My little servant Dorcas sits beside me while I write— I cannot persuade her to go to bed—she says it is so cold, she has her bed—three blankets & a No. Ca. Coverlet to cover with. I cannot help laughing at her—she dreads the cold so much.

19th Tuesday Last night the snow continued until the clouds were emptied—to what hour I cannot say—but this morning the sun rose as usual & it is now shining quite bright at 9 O'clock A.M. The tops of the houses & garden, yard, &c. all nicely covered with snow— I measured it in a level place, think it is at least four inches deep—what is called a dry light snow—the servants brought it into my room on their shoes, it did not melt—had it swept out—it left the floor & carpet dry— Dick walks through it & comes in with it—dry on the legs of his pants. I have more than fifty little chickens— Dorcas says they are all alive—they were in small coops protected on the N. side by old doors & boards—as beautiful as snow is, I soon tire of it— I think of every thing—how many human beings suffer from such weather—perhaps little clothing & little wood to keep up fires—many will suffer— I am thankful to know that nothing under my care need suffer— God has given me & them enough—far more than we deserve—raiment, food & fuel—what have we to complain of— nothing—nothing— We have enemies in the Northern people—but God can save us from them—if we deserve his protection:— but Oh Man is a dark & dreadful sinner— when God chastises a nation all have to suffer. Would that the goats could be discerned, by man, from the sheep—if they could we would have a purer people—for vice is so mean it will shrink from virtue—no matter how bold the offenders— Lord make thy people better, as wicked as many are—they still belong to thee while on earth & safe from the *Devil:*—after death they have no chance to plead— It is now dark—the snow had drifted deep on the north sides of the houses— I walked out to day after it had thawed where the sun shone on it—'twas not cold—my little chickens & turkeys looked well. This day I had snow packed into my dry well to try the experiment, see how it will keep—put pine straw at the bottom & covered it with rye straw. Will keep the door locked to keep the air out. Tom has a bad cold from runing in the snow. This was not what I call a beautiful snow—nature covered with sleet & the sunshining on it presents a briliant sight—this snow was all white & looked like a mountain winter scene. Yesterday I wrote to Mr. R.———to tell him Ben had beaten Louisa (nego phase of it)[8] & I did not think he should be allowed to do it—now I am sorry I noticed it—she may be as hard as he is. Now, Oh my Master, change this heart of mine & give it a new & better feeling is my prayer. I hope my Dear Mrs. Jones is better & all others who are in pain or distress— Lord be with my desolate sister & my suffering nephew—oh prepare us all to meet in a better land where none but pure spirits dwell. At night—19th March.

Wednesday 20th This is a tolerably pleasant day—though cold, the sun made it appear better than it was— Emma—Amy & Sally came unexpectedly to day—however I had a passable dinner for them—boiled the Old ham that Dick brought out on monday—beef steak, Irish potatoes—rice, homney, sausages— eggs—sweet potatoes & a boiled pudding— I was truely glad to see them & I feel the better for having seen them— Sylvia & myself had commenced making potatoe pudding— We put it aside until E——— left this afternoon & then finished. We succeeded in making beautiful paste for the pudding. *I thank thee Heavenly Father for all thy goodness— Oh make me thine—wholy thine.* This day new ground was planted in corn. To day E——— gave me one dollar for the eggs she took from Mrs. Rebecca Adams— Mrs. A——— told me to keep it in part pay for what she owed me for wheat & rye.

21 Thursday When I got up this morning I thought this promised to be a charming day— I have been out since breakfast & find it piercing cold—the sun is bright but Oh such a cold wind— cold enough it seems to me to destroy all that is left from the previous cold— I *said* this snow was too far North to anticipate a pleasant March. I sent Jim home with the carriage to

---

8. The Negro version of it—their story of what happened.

have two screws put in it—if I had known it was this cold I don't think I would have sent [him]. Mary complains a good deal of her back this morning. The sun shines uncommon bright—but the power of the wind mocks its powers—the traveler would wrap here in spite of Sol's rays. Oh God clothe the naked & feed the hungry—without thee we are poor—poor—creatures. Mrs. R. Adams was due me 2.07 cts.— I received yesterday 1.00 from E——— which reduces Mrs. A——— debt to 1.07 cts.—this will be easily cancelled. Here I obliged a poor neighbour & they have paid me back— I have not lost any thing by it—but felt much better for having done thus. I wish we had more such as Mrs. Adams—a good people is the strength of the nation.

22 Friday Was a pleasant day— I went down to see my friend Mrs. Jones—found her better— Mrs. Elkins was with her— Mr. Elkins called for his wife[9]— I did not like his looks but he improves on being in company with him—his face is broad—complexion pumpkin colour & poped eyes— I never could bear him in the pulpit & in fact his manners savours very little of the divine. Mrs. E——— is right good looking—but she must have had a desperate chance to take him—

23 remained this day—had my carriage at the door in the afternoon—but the clouds looked bad & I feared a spring gust—so concluded to stay until morning— I spent the evening & all the time pleasantly— Pauline & Laura are good girls, I do feel sorry to know how dependent they are.[10]

24 Sunday I left Mrs. Jones this morning & came to Beaulah Church—
morning Miss Hammond played on something[11]—but her music was too fast for church music—there were some good voices in the choir— I pray B——— may rise from her ashes & be a land mark yet for this region of country. Mr. B——— only tolerable to day—all we need is a more intelligent preacher with the true spirit—if we had such a one they would draw hearers, but *Organs* & *Mule chairs* never drew worth to any

---

9. W. B. Elkins, age forty-five, a Baptist minister living in Fairfield District in 1860, and his wife, Sarah, age twenty-three.

10. Grandchildren of Mrs. Jones, Pauline and Laura Scott, ages fifteen and fourteen respectively.

11. Sarah Hammond, seventeen-year-old daughter of Elias Hammond.

church.[12] The gospel in its purity does the work. After preaching I came home— Mr. Lykes spoke to me— Mill Creek wants a Depot on the R.R.— I do not wish it myself— I had rather see my Montgomery field converted into a gulph than to live to believe one bad act or example was ever committed on a spot of earth given for a Depot near me— I do despise meanness in any way—& if possible will never do any thing to make a place for it. I cannot change man—but I can avoid aiding what I believe would lead to wrong. Oh my God help me to do what is right in *thy sight*. This day received a letter from J. M. Adams asking me to go with them to Charleston in the morning—now this is a pretty way to act—how was I to arrange on sunday to get off before day monday— I said the notice was too short if I felt like going.

25th This is a bright morning— I am feeling very badly. I went to Emma's.

Tuesday 26 Left E. after breakfast. This is a cloudy unfavourable looking day. This day is rather warm—a good deal of wind. I pray for my country—trust that God will remember us in mercy—he knows our hearts as well as he knows the hearts of the fanatics— I am in the kitchen noticeing the baking of cakes— Rosanna struck up about three notes of a hymn— pretended she forgot I was near—*all deception*. I do wish God would punish deception with us at all times as he did with Saphira[13]—it is the only way to make man better, to visit him with punishments not soon forgotten— O what a deceitful race man is— I place him below the beasts—they know not right from wrong— Man does but prefers the wrong.

Wednesday 27th This is a morning of gentle rain—now 10 O'clock & the sun threatens to shine—heard Fanny Hopkins had been very sick— I hope 'tis temporary— Oh Lord prepare me for a better world & let me not live to witness war or know that there is any in the land— My God we go through sad trials for our negroes—they are very mean & unprincipled— I am willing my God should punish us for sins—we deserve it

---

12. A cacolet, a chair or litter consisting of two seats, one on each side of a pack animal such as a mule, hence a "mule chair."

13. Sapphira, wife of Ananias, a follower of the apostles, was struck dead for lying.

but let us fall in thy hands— Oh do not let the abolitionists, whom we have never meddled with, triumph over us—let them keep to themselves & let us do the same—punish us, but not by civil war— Oh God we are poor—poor—creatures.

28 of March— boiled the Old Ham brought out yesterday—Ada Hop-
Thursday kins—David—Amy—Miss Julia Rembert[14]—Mary Brooks, her two children, & Jane spent this day with me. I had one of the fine young goblers (yellow) of Mrs. Perry's for dinner—tongue—chicken pie—Asparagus—Irish & sweet potatoes—rice &c., &c.—ice cream for desert—soup— A mess of a dinner this was—every thing had an odd taste— sometimes my anger rises in spite of all I can do—what is the use of so much property when I can't get one thing cooked fit to eat—such a dinner—I am mad when I think how mean my negroes serve me— Oh my God help me to bear all of these crosses with more patience & Oh God fit me to leave them & take me to *Heaven*—there is nothing on *this earth* worth staying *one moment for* if we can only get to a better home—crosses after Crosses is all I realize on earth—the gleams of sunshine are so fleeting they are not worth the name. Jesus Master, I have lived to feel & know that there was a reality in the pleadings of the Revd Dr Baker of Austin, Texas[15]— Oh fervently he prayed—yes he must have had great, great trials or such pleadings never could have been poured forth. Oh how little man knows what is before him in this world—if at the age of 20—what I have passed through could have been placed before me—what could I have done but to put my hands on my mouth & laid down in the dust— Jesus Master, too small the number of those who feel what thou has done to save a sinking world:—sinking—yes we are all the time sinking—but for the hope in thee— blessed Master— I will try to cling to thee— What has saddened my heart so, this day—not a dinner alone—but to know the deceit of this world—the low standard of morals that do exist where there is so much enlightenment— Oh

---

14. Julia Rembert, seventeen-year-old daughter of Dr. James Rembert and sister of Adeline Rembert Hopkins.

15. William Baker, son of evangelist Daniel Baker, was pastor of Austin's Presbyterian Church. Critical of secession, after the Civil War he and most of his congregation associated with a northern wing of the church.

that I could do more good— I have tried example & advice to little purpose with my servants— Let me not expect to do what my master has not:—free this world from sin. 28 — Was a fine day.

29th Is a fine day— I have been as pettish as a child this day. Planted slips to day—some Randolph sent me—a few of my own.

30th Saturday I am ever angry with myself— I am so stubborn at times, then too yielding— I will not repeat the trifles that made me sin this day— I wonder if every heart is as unmanageable as *my own*, if so—do we not see more & more the blessings flowing from Revelations— Lord have mercy on *me*—30 day of March—pleasant—not very shining—finished planting corn at the field this day— I rode up to the field this morning—the Rye looks very well—the Oats has come up nicely, still quite short— I am thankful to know it is there & do hope it will be spared for the good of the stock. "Teach me thy way, O Lord, & lead me in a plain path." — Psalm XXVII—

Sunday 31st This is a briliant day—the wind is cool—only blowing moderately at present. Jim, Harry, Rosanna & John gone to Beaulah Church—this is a little strange—they have communion on the fifth sunday in March— I think this is all from the negroes—4th S. in April is usually communion sabbath.

April

"I never believed I should live to see my Country severed."

April 1st Day Cloudy this morning, the sun is trying to scatter the clouds. Heavenly Father I thank *thee* for thy protecting kindness. O Watch over our country & do what is best, for O my God we deserve nothing for ourselves, but thy goodness may save us. My Master put it into my heart to serve thee more & more— I do come far short of what I desire to be. Saturday 30th I received a letter from Harriet Russell of Marietta, Georgia. I am due G[oodwyn] Ross a letter. Now night— This day really has been an April day in aspect—we have had no rain—but some clouds & this evening every appearance of rain in showers, gentle, at a distance. Now the stars are bright & 'tis almost warm. May the month correspond with its first mild day. This first day of April 1861 I will write a new & more appropriate name for this place than I have hitherto found— Once I thought I would call it Hill Ed after the place where the different tribes of Israel united in friendship after their had been a temporary estrangement— Then I thought Mt. Trouble a more appropriate name— I felt there was little but trouble for me—now I have better feelings— will cast away the latter & call it Fontainebleau—this called from the french Fontaine de belle aue (The fountain of fine waters) the english of it—truely this is a place of fine waters—the section abounds in delightful, cool, clear springs of water. I took this from Mrs. Levert's book[1]— I know nothing of the french language.

April 2nd O God help me to subdue all my sins—the sin of anger is a terrible sin to contend with—a trifle often causes it to blaze sky high in a twinkling—then if God does not check it—it changes man or woman into a demon. Lord— Lord— help me from this slough of *Dispond* & fix me firmly on the rock

---

1. The first edition of Octavia Le Vert's *Souvenirs of Travel*, description of sights to be seen in Europe, appeared in 1857.

of *ages*. This is a foggy morning— I rather think 'twill rain— feels & looks spring. I now will take a walk in my garden— but the peaches are all destroyed, how badly I feel when I pass a peach tree, all gone—but what is the loss of peaches compared with many other losses—suppose we had been involved in a civil war & ere this had over all leveled in ashes— O Lord let me not murmur— I am sorry our once strong country is now severed & I believe forever—for I see no disposition in the stubborn North to yield any thing from advantage—& the South thought she would make the North succumb to her— *I* never thought it—& have ever thought we have began troubles for ourselves & cannot see how we are to be one tittle better off than we were—if all the South had gone united we might have maintained ourselves—but six states only—we are doomed I fear to be the division of the Old United States. O my God *help us—help us*— Let me not live to see these six states disagree & I fear it very much—man, unregenerate man can do nothing—his strength is in himself & he cannot stand without his God to guide & direct him. Last night I became anxious about Joe & Dorcas staying in Col——— I thought of Dyptheria—so very early, at the sight of day, I called Ned & sent him home on Roach to stop them from remaining in Col——— —they are to go up this day to have an operation on Dorcas' eye by Fair & Huo. Nature is putting forth her spring garb fast & this damp day will do a great deal in bringing up the corn— Oh I do hope there will be no more cold & frost. Only to think of Six divided States—how do others feel— I wish I knew the hearts of some of our leading men—it seemed to one we were greatly imposed on by the North—but if Vir., Ken., Ten., & No. Carolina could bear with it, we ought to have borne with all as long as they did. Now past 2 O['clock] P.M. Last night I dreamed I was in the Presbyterian church in Col———, sitting either in or near Mrs. C. Bryce's pew[2]— I thought Old Mrs. Bell sat at my right & young la-

---

2. Mrs. Campbell Bryce, wife of a well-to-do planter, lived at the southwest corner of Blanding & Pickens streets. One of the founders of Columbia's Wayside Hospital during the Civil War, she died in Philadelphia in 1901. Two other ladies mentioned in this dream sequence— Mrs. Bell and Mrs. Staunton—cannot be identified.

dies at my left— I soon missed Mrs. Bell— I turned to the left & saw Mrs. B. M. Palmer going from the pulpit up the aisle to the door—she was dressed in deep black with a black bonnet trimed very much—some one told me she had been up to the pulpit taking some bandages from Mr. P———['s] face—his health was feeble & he had to use them[3]— I thought Mr. P——— looked sunken near the eyes—then immediately I found myself alone—looking around, every one had left the church & gone out doors to hear the preaching—on my way out I saw Mother's old neighbour (long since dead), Mrs. Staunton, sitting on a chair looking very cheerful & happy— I proposed to go to the stand with her—she said not while Mr. P——— was there— I do not recollect her reasons, if any, for not doing so—is there any thing in dreams? After dinner I sent Tom to the field to get John to go with me to Sister's—he came running back with drops of sweat on his face saying the fence at the field was all on fire— I called to the servants—in a few minutes all left the yard—even a shorter time they were in leaving the church in *my* dream— I was left with only little Tom in my yard—Sylvia & an invalid mother in an out house—so I hope the dream is out—since writing this, Rosanna returns saying about sixty pannels of fence got burnt, they think they have subdued the fire— O Lord how uncertain is every thing in this world. It seems John alarmed the near neighbours who went to their assistance—while not one here either heard the noise or saw the smoke, there were eleven here & no one saw the smoke— I was thinking of riding to see my Sister, was in my bed room part of the time preparing to go.

April 3rd Late yesterday—indeed just after sun down—a terrific look-
Wednesday ing cloud rose in the West & wended its way round north & N. E.—it was a *dreadful Black* cloud—it came with a gust that filled the air with dust—some lightning & thunder— Such a cloud must have been awful where the main body exhausted itself—it had so pretty much before the rain came

---

3. Benjamin M. Palmer (1818–1902), Charleston native and ardent secessionist, was pastor of Columbia's Presbyterian Church from 1843 to 1855, also serving briefly on the faculty of the Theological Seminary before moving to New Orleans in 1856.

on here—however we had a plenty of rain from [it]—the rain continued at intervals through the night, so did the lightning— This morning is very cloudy, every thing very wet—the wind is getting up & there is quite a change in the air—last night was uncomfortably warm, now quite cool— I trust 'twill not grow colder through the day—if it does while everything is so wet, we may bid adieu to our strawberries. The beds are now white with blossoms & many apple trees are full of blooms—these are nothing if our country was only settled down quietly— I still fear So. Ca. cannot be pleased— I do not love her disposition to cavil at every move— My heart has never been in this breaking up of the Union—but if we could be united lovingly & firmly, I will cling to my dear native land—for I love my country—but I hate contention:—too many are waiting for the loaves & fishes, South as well as North— Oh we lack *true religion*— such as the blessed saviour left us in his last *will*. Sunday will be our communion Sabbath at the P. C——— in Col———, I wish I could feel like being there to commemorate the legacy— O My Master make me thine in heart, in acts outwardly & in every way—help me to devote my life to thee—all thou requirest is purity— What is more lovely. Lord, save Our Country!!!

Thursday 4th This morning damp, cold, cloudy, the sun tries to shine. I feel very sad to day. The news in the papers from Charlotte, No. Ca———, bears me down—down— Col. Myers had out houses burned— Mr. Elms & some other persons[4]—we know not what moment we may be hacked to death in the most cruel manner by our slaves— Oh God devise a way for us to get rid of them quietly & let us all be better christians— Oh God save us—save us—poor worms of the dust we are— I don't know how I feel—feel as if there was nothing on earth to cheer me— Oh my God help me up—help all thy desponding children. I think a desperate state of things exist at the South—our negroes are far more knowing than many will acknowledge— I had a little negro girl about the house to say to me the other day—'twas a sin for big ones like them to say sir to Mass Thomas & Mass Whitfield &

---

4. William Myers, age fifty-six, a wealthy planter, lived at the "crossroads" on Horrell Hill. Mr. Elms cannot be identified.

little ones like them (T. & W.—a babe & a little boy)[5]—now if black children have this talk what are we to expect from grown negroes—this same little girl has told me I did not know how my negroes hated white folks & how they talked about *me*. Perhaps I trust too much in man—no, I have *no faith* in *man* who will not fall on his knees & plead for aid from above—we can do nothing of ourselves. I have just closed a letter to my Sister Mrs. P. J. Brevard of North Carolina. Vir., K., T., & N. C. still cling to the Old U. S. of America.

Friday 5th A tolerably good day— I left the S. Hills in time to get to Cabin branch a little after 12—Midday—in the afternoon—Fanny—John & myself put seventy two new hams in bags. 72. Hams. & left hanging without any bags eighty seven. 87. I had to count these looking up— I am sure there are that many hanging—there may be a few over this no. but not under it— John made them out three over what I did. These hams seem to be fine in quality, some few quite large. Mr. R.——— went to Col to day, he returned quite sick—after bathing and going to bed a while he got relief & after supper got up & sat & talked with Miss Jackson[6]—his wife & myself—he told us it was discovered to day that the three City [fire] engines had been rendered useless by cutting them & putting rocks in them—was not God good to let this be known!!! Oh My God—here is proof to us we are on a vessel ready to be cut loose in a moment & hurled into eternity— O Lord thou hast saved us in this instance— Oh save us now & forever from wars—change the hea[r]ts of man towards his brother man & suffer us not to be such beasts of the forest as we are—trying our best to bring trouble on this once blessed land—yes, blessed until the blinded politicians sought mischief by bringing the barbarous African to this civilized country— O Lord forgive those who were so blinded & heal all our ill feelings— My God we do feel & know all things are in thy hands— Oh save us—save us. My Heavenly Father be with my poor desolate Sister this

---

5. Thomas David Hopkins (1860–1888), eldest son of Adeline Rembert and David Hopkins, and Whitfield Brooks (born in 1858), son of Mary Goodwyn Adams and John Hampden Brooks, brother of the man who caned Senator Sumner.

6. Louisa Jackson, the forty-year-old daughter of a nearby farmer.

night—prepare us both for Heaven & take us quickly from our troubles.

Saturday 6th I got up after spending one night in deep trouble— I wondered if our people were to be spared in the dark world to see another sun rise. We have been spared, blessed Jesus— *Oh extend thy loving kindness to us a while longer—spare us good Lord!!* This has been a cloudy day & now after dark the wind is high & it certainly is much colder. I fear for the strawberries & Apples—this night will try them & all the corn that is up— My God be not angry with us, *thy poor servants*, I have loved the laws of my God & my Country—if they are broken I had no part nor lot in doing it—but I must now go with her if she is wrong. To day I gave out shorts[7]— I gave each family one tin cup full round, then threw in two cup over to each family, to each single old man I gave four pints & sent a little lard to each family— I emptied the jar that was in the new meat house—still left 13 jars not touched & one large jar of Old lard for greasing the shop bellows & harness.

7th Sunday We had a great deal of rain through last night & all this morning—it slacked about 11 A.M.—still cloudy—cold & sprinkling a little occasionally— Now 20 m[inutes] of 2 O'Clock—indeed we have a variable April, as well as the fall & winter—some say the sun is loosing his power to warm— I notice when he is permitted to shine there does not seem any diminution of heat—but it seems the winds & clouds have contended with his power over since Cessession. I cannot believe the South did right to break up our Union— She ought to have been united, then we could have kept back the No——— until the S——— could feel 'twas necessary to draw off. I am sorry to say I do despise the principles of the Northern Republicans & I pray God will restrain them & teach them to pray for *themselves* & let *God* judge us for he is our great Judge & Master—not the trifling pigmies of the North— Southerners have worshiped you Northerners a long time—it was sufficient to say such an one was from the N———, such a young lady educated in P———, such a young man got his profession in N——— Colleges, &c., &c.—every governess—from the N——— must come—&

---

7. The part of milled grain next finer than bran, often called middlings.

so the fools of the S——— have worshiped all that came N——— of Dixon's line. We all have legions of bad feelings ever rising—my feelings to those who wish to trample us to earth is wrong, I know, when viewed by My Master—but Oh God thou knowest we tried to do right & feel right—all we got in turn was hatred— Lord forgive me & make me thine— I love *my God*— My blessed Saviour—but *I cannot love those who hate us.*

Monday 8 The bad weather continues—now near 2 O'clock P. M. & 'tis raining quite hard—such weather adds bad feelings to our sad hearts— Oh Lord save us!! save us!! but I see nothing to hope for— Garden— This day Joe & Dick have replanted Water melons, Cucumbers & Squashes— I think it is a bad time for it, the rains will beat the ground close & if it turns off dry bake the earth & prevent their getting through easily, just had a flash of lightning & a roll of thunder— I do hope this may be the last shower— I call this disagreeable, cold rain—my poor little chickens & two feeble little turkeys, I wish the sun could shine to dry your little bodies. Hams. This day two new hams & one new Shoulder came out in the cart—about three pecks of red slips.[8] Ned brought these. Had one of these hams boiled for dinner— Rosanna half boiled it—147 links of sausages still hanging at home.

9 Tuesday went to Jane's— Heard sad news—a fleet was thought to be approaching Charleston—the 6th regiment was ordered to Charleston, some went to day— Dr Ray's company will go tomorrow— Randy came up to bid his parents good bye— even James H——— was overcome—he could not speak when I bid him good bye. Lord save our *Dear—Dear Country—this blessed land.*

10 Wednesday This morning's bright sun shine cheered me & Janie's note bringing the glad tidings that all was well in Charleston, after hearing it, I felt as if I could shout glory! glory! Oh what a charming day this is—beautiful! & God's goodness in watching over us makes it more lovely still. Lord *thou hast* remembered us in thy mercy. Now many sad hearts will be turned to joy:— Many who were bathed in tears yesterday— will be smiling through the dew drops of affection.

---

8. Sweet potato slips.

Thursday the 11th Early this morning it was drizling—it then cleared off, we now have a pretty day— How thankful I am—my Country is still spared— Lord save us & make us better— I pray that all things will be ordered for peace. How changeable my feelings are—sometimes buoyed with a hope of good times (this is momentary), then I can see & hear nothing to hang my hopes on— Why are they stubborn about the forts if they have any thought of reconciliation. Flour— I took a bag of flour to Randy on Tuesday—this leaves ten bags of good flour up stairs. Gardening—planted Okra in the new ground this 11 of April— Planted red slips in the Old cow pen yesterday 10th— Hams— Now have two new hams & one Shoulder in the meat house.

Friday 12th Left one of these hams to be boiled this morning when I left for Sister's—12th I have been to Sister's—sat with her about two hours—returned by the deserted Village.[9] Friday afternoon— Now cloudy & we have had a shower since three o'clock.

Saturday 13th This is a bright, warm windy day. We had lightning last night & some rain, a good sprinkle yesterday about four O'clock in the afternoon. Tomattos seed in the ground this morning—some beet seed. The Tomatto seed Sister gave me I sowed in a short row by the East palling of the garden. Oh Father of mercies, I thank thee that we are still safe, still preserved by thy *Almighty power.* Frank & Munson go this afternoon to Columbia— I lent Munson fifty cts. 50 cts. loaned. Spent Sunday at home—had two little negroes sick—sent for Dr Taylor[10]—he came in the afternoon & gave me the news from Charleston— Said Ft. Sumpter had been taken— Col. Anderson surrendered—he lost 9 or ten men— So. Ca. not one— Oh my God I thank thee for spareing blood here— Lord 'twas hard the citizens of Charleston should be rendered so miserable by that Fort— I am thankful it is no longer there a terror, but Oh my God we may still tremble for we have enemies in our midst— Oh God send them away to a land they love better than ours & Oh devise a way for our peace & safety & let the praise be thine—for who can doubt but thou didst so order it. A few months ago & 'twas said man could not take Ft. Sumpter un-

---

9. The summer colony of Adams Hill.
10. Simeon Taylor, age fifty, a resident of Lower Richland.

less walking over five or ten thousand dead—it has been taken—& not *one* life lost of those who aided in taking it— My God the work is thine & if we serve the[e] truthfully thou wilt save us— Oh save us & make us still a united contented people—we wish no ill to the North—all we ask is that they leave us to ourselves or gra[n]t us privileges & laws that will protect us— My God be with all thy dear Children— Oh how desolate many are now— Husbands & sons gone to the scenes of war—to save their [country].

14 of April Sunday was a good day.

15 This is a very windy day—clouds brewing. One of my poor neighbours sat with me this morning—two of her sons gone to Charleston in the Sixth Regiment—it left last friday or thursday, the 11th or 12th— The papers say Mr. Edmund Ruffin fired the first shot on Ft. Sumpter.[11] O Lord let the N. & S. now compromise & shed no more blood. This book is closed with the beginning of the war of 1861— I never believed I should live to see my Country severed & that by those who pretend to be the best people— My God save this Country & do not let me live to see misery in this once favoured land. *Amen.* Col. Anderson of Ft. Sumpter surrendered on saturday the 13th of April 1861. Now dark & it is raining quite hard—rain began to fall soon after sundown.

---

11. Virginian Edmund Ruffin (1794–1865), agriculturalist, publisher, and ardent secessionist, was given the honor of firing the first shot at Fort Sumter from an installation on Morris Island; however, legend to the contrary, this was *not* the first shot fired in the Civil War.

Epilogue
After the War

Keziah Brevard experienced the turmoil of the 1860s firsthand, and at the close of the Civil War Sherman's men burned at least two of her homes, Cabin Branch and Mill Place. The status of the Columbia town house is unclear. Some sources indicate it survived the fire of February 1865; others say it did not. Since Keziah re-recorded her deed to that property the following year, she obviously thought that, whatever its condition, it had some value. Alwehav was vandalized by invading troops, but not burned. In the entrance hall of present-day Oldfield stands a handsome secretary with one drawer missing—taken, it is said, by Sherman's "bummers." All of her slaves were, of course, set free, and whatever railroad stock she held became virtually worthless.

As if these economic losses were not enough, in the late 1860s Keziah had to deal with a family controversy following the death of half sister Sarah Hall, who had been plagued by mental problems for several decades. Unlike Joseph Brevard, Keziah's husband, "Sister" never was placed in a mental institution; however, in 1851 a local court declared her to be legally insane and put her finances in the hands of a committee headed by nephew and neighbor James Hopkins Adams. Prior that time Sarah's stepfather, James Hopkins, attended to such matters; following the death of Adams in 1861, Keziah assumed responsibility.

Yankee troops apparently burned Sarah's home (Bellewood), and records of Columbia lawyer Fitz William McMaster on deposit at the South Caroliniana Library indicate that in 1866 she was eager to rebuild. Even though Sarah was seventy-five years of age and mentally disturbed, this grand dame still was able to carry on a spirited and lucid correspondence with McMaster. Her letters reflect little appreciation for Keziah's hospitality, characterizing her half sister as "the greatest tyrant" and complaining bitterly that the latter's increasing deafness made her a virtual prisoner in her own room. Meanwhile, relatives in Louisiana—Keziah and Ella, daughters of Jesse Goodwyn, the same two nieces who would inherit part of Keziah's estate—cautioned McMaster that "Aunt Hall" was much too old to undertake any construction program, a view probably shared by Keziah as well. McMaster did, however, purchase furniture for his client at her request.

Then early in 1867 Sarah died, leaving no will. In November of that year, Keziah presented McMaster with a modest bill ($1,591.20) for corn and fodder that she supplied to her half sister's plantation between 1846 and 1862. Soon after that, B. F. Wharton, husband of Keziah Goodwyn, one of the Louisiana nieces, submitted a huge claim for $37,859, a sum he said represented money (plus interest) that Mrs. Hall had loaned to James Hopkins, Keziah's father.[1] Although McMaster had evidence indicating Sarah actually owed her stepfather nearly $4,000 at the time of his death, Wharton stoutly maintained that Mrs. Hall had "saved" Hopkins in the 1830s. Laban L. Tomkies, the husband of the other Louisiana niece, took a dim view of such claims, informing his brother-in-law Wharton, quite frankly, that they probably were invalid. Wharton, although distressed by this rift with Keziah, "one of the best of women," stuck to his guns, asserting that she simply had forgotten much that had transpired through the years, and continued to insist that whatever assets existed should be split among three heirs: his wife, Mrs. Tomkies, and Keziah.

There matters stood until November 1870 when a surprise claimant appeared seeking his share, one George A. Hall, a descendant of Sarah's husband. McMaster subsequently informed Richland County officials that the entire estate did not exceed $3,500; however, since no inventory exists, it is unclear whether anyone ever got anything. This was, of course, merely another chapter in the mad scramble of the immediate postwar era for dollars.

Perhaps the most interesting by-product of this entire affair was a chance remark contained in a letter Wharton forwarded to McMaster in February 1868. After conceding that "Aunt Brevard" was "one of the best of women" and admitting that their differences might end in court proceedings, he added that Keziah clearly was "not a business woman." Nothing could have been further from the truth. Despite

---

1. Through some obscure logic, Wharton also sought to collect $21,752 from the estate of James Hopkins Adams and $19,625 from that of Jesse H. Goodwyn, who also was involved at some point with management of Mrs. Hall's finances. In addition, Wharton was irked by Keziah's bill, vowing in a letter to McMaster that she never would have presented it "had she not been put up to it, by someone well known to yourself." This is perhaps a veiled reference to English Hopkins.

reduced income and the rough years of Reconstruction, this indomitable widow carried on amazingly well, leasing her lands to tenants and using that income to pay taxes.

According to tradition, Keziah G. H. Brevard never sold a slave or a tree, and an inventory following her death in 1886 indicates the latter was essentially true, although she evidently had disposed of her city residence. And, in what may have been an "arrangement," in 1869–1870 she sold fourteen acres of land to the heirs of A. S. Rawlinson, her deceased overseer, and acquired from them the Goodwyn family cemetery where she and her husband are buried. James Hopkins left his daughter about 2,300 acres of land; she devised nearly three times as much to her heirs—6,710 acres. (For the text of her will, see Appendix A.)

Keziah Brevard thus presents the fascinating picture of one Southerner who swam against the tide—successfully. Before 1860 this plantation mistress operated with consummate skill in an agricultural realm dominated by men. Can anyone, for example, picture Emma Holmes or Mary Chestnut bundling up a dying black youngster and taking him for a ride in her carriage, personally parceling out foodstuffs and clothing to slaves, or collecting lard at hog killing time? After the war Keziah performed equally well (one might even say spectacularly) at a time when others, both male and female, struggled amid storm-tossed waves.

And does this diary disclose clues to Keziah's formula for success? Perhaps it does. It reveals great attention to detail—counting pennies, even half-pennies, and keeping a record of supplies given to slaves, wine bottled, and preserves put by—and a spirit of true independence, shaping one's own life as much as possible, even if the price was many lonely hours. It would, upon reflection, be difficult to devise a better recipe for riding out the turmoil of Reconstruction and the hard years that came in its wake. One suspects that many farm households, also often headed by widows, followed similar precepts during the dark decades of the late nineteenth century.

Perhaps the most striking fact is how little the Civil War actually affected the day-to-day life of this remarkable woman. There were, of course, sweeping economic changes. Before 1865 Keziah G. H. Brevard, with the help of overseer Abraham Rawlinson, ruled two hundred slaves. After that time English Hopkins replaced Rawlinson, some slaves became tenants, crops were planted and harvested, seasons passed, and life seemed to move in familiar channels. What we need is a diary similar to that of 1860–1861 to tell us how *un*familiar some of those channels actually were.

Regrettably—and this is quite understandable—neither Keziah nor most of her contemporaries were eager to document a postwar world filled with unsettling trends and new ideas. Perhaps, if Keziah had adjusted less well, today we might have another slim volume of her thoughts and observations during the tumultuous 1860s and 1870s. But that was not to be. With the end of slavery, several reasons for keeping a household journal vanished. The task of chronicler thus fell to those reaping the special benefits of the new era, and an aging plantation mistress existing quietly in the Sand Hills of central South Carolina was not among that number.

Appendixes

Appendix A
Will of Keziah Goodwyn Hopkins Brevard

The State of South Carolina

In the name of God, Amen. I, Keziah G. H. Brevard, of Richland
County, in the state aforesaid, being of sound mind and disposing
memory, but weak in body and realizing the uncertainty of human
life, do hereby make, publish, and declare this my *Last Will and Testament*, hereby revoking all other wills at any time heretofore made by
me, and also declaring this will to be as well the expression of my
own wishes as to the disposition of property herein mentioned after
my death, as also the execution of the powers conferred upon me in
and by the last will and testament of my father, James Hopkins, deceased—

Item I. I wish all my just debts and funeral expenses paid out of
property not hereinafter specifically disposed of.

Item II. All that tract of land in Richland County, state aforesaid,
eight or nine miles below Columbia, containing two thousand, four
hundred and ten (2410) acres, more or less, and bounded (now or
lately) as follows: north by lands of Alfred Wallace, Adam Hunter,
and Mrs. Yates; south by Alfred Wallace and lands formerly of Gen.
Wm. Hopkins' estate, and east by Paul G. Chappell, south-east by
Rawls, and west by lands of Alfred Wallace and W. B. Nash—I di-
vide into three shares, one share whereof I devise to my niece, Keziah
E. Wharton, for and during the term of her natural life, with the remainder to such of my own next of kin as the said Keziah E. Wharton
may appoint by her last will and testament duly executed, and in
default of such appointment, then to the nearest of my own blood
relations.

Item III. One other third or share of the Bluff Lands herein above
described in the second item of this will, I give and devise to my
niece Ella V. Tomkins [sic], for and during the term of her natural life
with the remainder at her death to her children then surviving, the

issue of any deceased child to take by representation the share of such their deceased parent—

Item IV. The remaining third or other equal share of said Bluff lands, I give and devise to Caroline H. Smith, John Ross, and James Ross, share and share alike, for and during the term of their respective lives, with remainder, as to the share of each, to their children surviving them, the issue of any deceased child to take by representation the share of such their deceased parent— If any one of said life-tenants in this item mentioned, die without issue then surviving, the share of such one to pass to their nephews and nieces, nearest of kin.

Item V. I give and devise to Amy Hopkins and Sally Hopkins, to them and the heirs of their body forever, my Jesse Goodwyn and Myers tracts of land aggregating between five and six hundred acres of land, more or less, purchased by me before the war from Col. John Hopkins, and lying south-east of the Cabin Branch or old Hopkins tract. The devises of this item named are the daughters of the late Gen. Wm Hopkins, of Richland County, state aforesaid.

Item VI. I give and devise to James Hopkins (who is a brother of David Hopkins and English Hopkins, both hereinafter mentioned) for and during the term of his natural life, with remainder to his children surviving him (the issue of any deceased child to take by representation the share of such their deceased parent) five hundred (500) acres of the Cabin Branch tract, or tract marked "D" in survey and plat of Thos. C. Veal, C. E. & S., February 12, 1857, to be laid off at the Eastern End of said tract, by a line running from "stake 3xn in ditch" on south-east boundary to such point on the northern boundary as will make five hundred acres to the east of said line in said tract "D."

Item VII. I give and devise unto Mrs. Mary L. Jones, for and during the term of her natural life, with remainder to her surviving children (the issue of any deceased child to take by representation the share of such their deceased parent) the tract of land marked "B" on said Veal Survey of 1857, to which shall be added on its Southern boundary so much of tract "D" of said survey as will make in the aggregate five hundred (500) acres, the line to be run from the southwest corner of said tract "B" to such point on the southern or southern line of said tract "D" as will give between the said line and the

James Hopkins line in item sixth directed to be run, enough land to make with tract "B" said five hundred acres.

Item VIII. I give and devise to English Hopkins for and during the term of his natural life, with remainder to his children surviving him (the issue of any deceased child to take by representation the share of such their deceased parent) five hundred (500) acres of my Cabin Branch tract to be taken out of tracts "C," "D," "E," and "F" (one, or more, or all) on said Veal Survey and Plat, as follows, that is to say so much of said tracts as lies on the west of the Mary L. Jones line run as directed in the seventh item above, and to the eastward of a line to be run from the Stateburg and Columbia line road, south down the old road on the Veal Survey into tract "E," then along the dotted line to where it (the dotted line) passes from tract "E" into tract "C," and thence to run from such point of intersection to such other point on the western, southern, or southeastern boundary of the said survey as will give five hundred acres to pass under this item of my will.

Item IX. I give and devise to David Hopkins for and during the term of his natural life, with remainder to his children him surviving (the issue of any deceased child to take by representation the share of such their deceased parent) all the remainder of the Cabin Branch tract, or tracts "C" and "E," not hereinabove devised, to which shall be added so much of the Addison tract adjoining (purchased by me from Fred. Lykes before the war) as will make five hundred acres of land to pass under the devise in this section.

Item X. If the land devised to David Hopkins in the ninth item of this will shall fail to aggregate the five hundred acres desired, the devises in the sixth, seventh, eighth, and ninth items hereof shall be so reduced in quantity that an equal quantity of land shall be received by James Hopkins, Mary L. Jones, English Hopkins, and David Hopkins under this will, and the lines in said items directed to be run, shall be so run as to carry out the directions of this item.

Item XI. I give and devise my Sand Hill Home Place, supposed to contain about eighteen hundred acres, to be divided equally, share and share alike, between the following persons and classes, to each one-fourth, viz. (1) Walker Adams, (2) the daughters of Mary Brooks, late wife of J. Hampden Brooks, (3) the daughters of Jane Brooks, present wife of J. H. Brooks, (4) the daughters of Carry Le Conte—to be held and enjoyed by said persons and classes for and during the term of their natural lives with remainders to their issue surviving them, and in default thereof, to their survivors—

Item XII. I nominate and appoint David Hopkins, English Hopkins, and John Ross executors of this my last will and testament— In witness whereof I have hereunto signed my name and affixed my seal this thirtieth day of September in the year of Our Lord, one thousand eight hundred and eighty five, and have at the same time signed my name on the margin of the first sheet upon which this will is written.

(signed) Keziah G. H. Brevard.

Witnesses:
  R. T. Reese
  A. P. Smith
  Robt. W. Shand

Executed September 30, 1885
Probated November 23, 1886

Appendix B
Partial Inventory of Estate

At the time of her death, Keziah had $4,461 in a bank account and $122.50 in her purse. She owned five hundred shares of City of Columbia bonds ($300), twenty-three shares of Charlotte, Columbia & Augusta Railroad stock ($805), and $84.55 in Columbia municipal scrip said to be worth $50. Her personal wealth also included $147.53 in rent collections, a note of "Miss Hopkins" for $227.26, and personal possessions appraised at $1,570.50—a total of $7,683.79. The partial inventory that follows does not include paintings, some silver, and various items earmarked for Louisiana relatives, as well as an old sideboard, a book case, two rocking chairs, and six "high" presses (total value $29) that, for some reason, the appraisers listed separately.

Two (2) Head of Horses	$250.00
Five (5) Head [of] Cattle	35.00
Vehicles	150.00
One (1) Carriage & Harness	15.00
One (1) old Carriage	15.00
One (1) Wagon & gear	15.00
One (1) Plowstock & plows	2.00
One (1) Garden Plow	1.50
Provender	483.50[1]
130 bu. corn more or less at 30 ¢ Bus.	39.00
1,400 lbs. Fodder more or less at 50 ¢ pr. 100 lbs.	7.00
13 Sax cotton seed meal	13.00
½ Bbl. sugar	10.00
⅔ Bbl. Flour more or less	3.00
House hold Furniture	
Three (3) Bureaus	45.00
Seven (7) Bedsteads	50.00
Three (3) washstands	20.00
Five (5) pr. Brass Firedogs	35.00

---

1. This figure ($483.50) actually is the total to that point, not an appraisal of provender as indicated.

One (1) sewing Machine	20.00
Three (3) Low Presses	4.00
Seven (7) Feather Beds	45.00
Six (6) Mattresses	20.00
Eight (8) Pillows	4.00
Seven (7) Bolsters	7.00
Four (4) Rugs	20.00
Eight (8) carpets	100.00
Seven Trunks & contents	50.00
One (1) clock	1.00
Two (2) Dining Tables	10.00
Six (6) Pine Tables	6.00
One (1) new Piano	150.00
One (1) old Piano	10.00
One (1) Invalid chair	20.00
Seventeen (17) walnut chairs	8.50
Six (6) Straw Bottom chairs	3.00
One (1) arm chair	1.50
One (1) Hatrack	3.00

Parlor Furniture

Two (2) Mohair & one (1) silk sofa	60.00
Three (3) Whatnots	20.00
One (1) marble top center table	15.00
Two (2) Plush & one (1) silk arm chair	25.00
Five (5) Mohair & two (2) silk chairs	20.00
Two (2) Mohair settees	10.00

Miscellaneous

2 tin water cans	.50
2 tin slop bucket	.50
1 stone foot tub	.75
3 Pitchers & Bowles	5.00
4 Brass Fenders	5.00
Lot china & crockery & glassware	50.00
6 Chandeliers	20.00
2 Lamps	1.50

Silverware and Jewelry

11 Plated forks	2.00
Seven Plated Teaspoons	1.00
1 doz. silver Forks	10.00
1 doz. silver Tablespoons	10.00
2 little silver spoons	1.00
1 doz. silver "T" spoons	6.00
1 Butter Knife	1.50
Silver coffee pot	15.00
1 silver Teapot	15.00
1 silver sugar dish	10.00
1 silver spoon bowl	15.00
1 " watch	5.00
1 " cup	10.00
2 pr. gold spectacles	5.00
1 " steel "	.50
1 Gold Breast pin, jet setting	2.00
1 Cameo & Pearl Breast Pin	10.00
1 Bas Breast Pin, Pearl & jet	3.00

Cutlery

1 doz. celuloid dinner Knives, carver & forks	2.00
1 doz. Roger dinner Knives, carver & forks	8.50
1 " " BKst " , " " "	6.00
5 old Knives	1.00
16 steel forks	2.00
6 Plated candlesticks	5.00
Kitchen Furniture &c.	10.00
[total]	$1,570.50[2]

---

2. The total, marked over and much revised, should be $1,578.25.

Sources

Columbia City Directory. Columbia, 1859.

Columbia Directory. Columbia, 1860.

Daily Southern Guardian. Columbia, 1860–1861.

Hopkins, Laura Jervey. *Lower Richland Planters: Hopkins, Adams, Weston, and Related Families of South Carolina.* Columbia, 1976.

Southern Christian Advocate. Columbia, 1860–1861.

Southern Presbyterian Review. Columbia, 1860–1861.

Unpublished Materials, South Carolina Department of Archives and History
    Federal Census Schedules, 1850, 1860.
    Richland County Probate Court Records, 1830–1886.
    Patient Treatment Records, South Carolina State Hospital, 1828–1853.

Personal Papers
    Brevard-McDowell Papers, Southern Historical Collection, Chapel Hill, NC.
    McMaster Family Papers, South Caroliniana Library, Columbia, SC.

Index